WITHDRAWN
NDSU

THE COLOUR BAR IN EAST AFRICA

THE COLOUR BAR IN EAST AFRICA

NORMAN LEYS, M.B., D.P.H.
Maclean
Author of *Kenya* and *A Last Chance in Kenya*.

"For if thou altogether holdest thy peace at this time, then shall there enlargement and deliverance arise from another place ; but thou and thy father's house shall be destroyed ; and who knoweth whether thou art come to the kingdom for such a time as this ?"

NEGRO UNIVERSITIES PRESS
NEW YORK

Originally published in 1941
by The Hogarth Press, London

Reprinted in 1970 by
Negro Universities Press
A Division of Greenwood Press, Inc.
Westport, Connecticut

SBN 8371-3609-1

Printed in United States of America

CONTENTS

	PAGE
Preface	7
Abbreviations	11

CHAPTER		
I.	Explanatory	13
II.	How Colour Bars Arose	22
III.	Land	31
IV.	The Squatters	41
V.	As Seen From the Other End	49
VI.	How the People Live	60
VII.	European Taxation and Related Matters	80
VIII.	Mines	91
IX.	Politics	101
X.	Education	125
XI.	The Background	141
XII.	The Way Out	150

PREFACE

FIFTY odd years ago Lord Lugard was a subaltern, on leave from his regiment in India. He spent the time in that part of Central Africa, then only half explored, that now is called Nyasaland. The only Europeans who were living, at that time, in the country north-west of Lake Nyasa were a few clerks and storekeepers belonging to a Scottish trading company and some half-dozen Scottish missionaries, who had established themselves athwart one of the last to be used of the routes over which Arab slave caravans travelled to the coast. When Lugard arrived he found a minor war going on between those men and the Arabs. He joined in the fighting and was wounded, as also was the manager of the trading company. (That was the first battle of Karonga. The second was fought in September 1914 with the Germans. Next day Lord Lugard cabled us his congratulations.) The loss of the battle by the Arabs brought their authority in those parts to an end, and the chiefs of the two tribes in the district, in gratitude for the deliverance of their people, signed a document that conveyed the land of the tribes to the trading company. Such a reward would be considered excessive nowadays. But there are many other estates in East Africa, that comprise thousands of square miles, that were acquired less justifiably, and far more cheaply.

Soon after those events the company tried to get a Royal Charter, failed to do so, and got into financial

PREFACE

difficulty. So it sold the land in North Nyasa, that had and has a population of about 60,000, to the powerful Chartered Company of South Africa, now the British South Africa Company. And when, a little later, a British Administration was set up in Nyasaland, the claim of the B.S.A. Co. to the land was duly recognized. A few years later still the Government imposed a tax of a farthing an acre on privately owned land, and the B.S.A. Co., being the largest landowner in the country, paid several thousand pounds a year in the tax for many years, though it had practically no revenue from the land. When I spent a few months in North Nyasa fifteen years after that first battle of Karonga, I found that chiefs and people had no idea that their land belonged to anyone but themselves—laughed at it in fact. So the matter stood. And so, I might have written, it still stands, if I had not happened to meet a man who used to be in the Colonial Office. He told me that a few years ago the Colonial Office made an agreement with the B.S.A. Co., by which the company conveyed the land to the Government but retained the mineral rights. In return the Government repaid the company the money that in past years it had paid in land tax. The point of the story is that that last episode is nowhere publicly recorded. I learned of it purely by chance, and if I had not chanced to learn of it, I might have made the misstatement in this book that the North Nyasa District is the property of the B.S.A. Co.

Again, until 1940 the population of Kenya was stated in official reports to be three millions, or rather more. But in the last annual report, that was published when this book was nearly finished, the African population is given as 3,365,000. Curiously enough the numbers of Europeans and Asiatics, that used to be given with precision, appear in the same report as 20,000 and 50,000 respectively. No explanation is given of these changes, and no real reason for them can exist, since there has been no census. The truth of the matter is that we have no reliable vital statistics for any East African country. None is possible, since nowhere is the registration of births compulsory. So the estimates of infant mortality some people have made, which when trustworthy are the best of all tests of social health, are simply guesses. (Sir Philip Mitchell is reported to have begun to have exact records kept in Uganda, which if true is much to his credit.) Nevertheless readers may, I believe, take the official vital estimates that will be quoted in the book as roughly correct, except when made with some ulterior end. What happens then may be judged by this incident. Archdeacon Owen, whose services to Africans it would be impertinence in me to praise, attacks specific injustices rather than the policy which, in my conviction, makes them inevitable. Knowing what a heavy burden the hut and poll tax in Kenya is, he saw one way to lighten it by getting the age at which people become liable to pay the tax raised from sixteen to eighteen, which is the age at which Europeans in Kenya become liable to pay their poll tax. For years he kept pointing to this obvious and unjust discrimination. In the end he won, and the age limit was raised to eighteen. But in the next, and in succeeding years, the total yield of the tax remained the same.

The case of the ownership of about a tenth of Nyasaland, and the facts about vital statistics in Kenya, though otherwise dissimilar, are raised here because they both show how difficult accurate information of certain kinds is to come by in East African affairs.

PREFACE

On certain other matters, in regard to produce of all sorts, and of course money, abundant and exact information is available. So that, for example, we know that the monthly income of the average miner of gold in Kenya is 10s. 7d., but do not know how many of his children survive their first year of life. I can only plead that in these pages I have taken great pains to be as accurate as possible.

The critics to whom I owe most thanks are my wife, my daughter, my sister Helen, who also read the proofs for me at a time when I was prevented by illness, my publisher, Leonard Woolf, and a friend of my youth, H. N. Brailsford. This book is merely a small contribution to the account of Imperial affairs that is contained in the books these two men have written.

ABBREVIATIONS

D.O., District Officer, the magistrate and tax collector in charge of one of the administrative units into which every British African country is divided.

N.A. A Native Authority is the child of two parents. Its mother, now deceased, was the governing authority of a tribe, whether embryonic and indeterminate or embodied in a recognized chief or council or both. Its father was a British Government. In law it is a subordinate agency of that Government. In West Africa, some N.A.s remain the traditional bodies they were a century and more ago. Elsewhere the traditional has been adapted or transformed. But nearly always some degree of semblance and continuity with the past survives.

N.A.D. In the two Rhodesias and Kenya, where all industry except the growing of food crops is in the hands of Europeans and European interests predominate, the administration of Districts that are occupied by African tribes, together with their District Officers, is directed by a Native Affairs Department.

CHAPTER I

EXPLANATORY

MOST people know that in South Africa skilled jobs are reserved for Europeans. And when people speak of a colour bar they mean whatever it is that prevents Africans from doing skilled and better-paid work, whether it be an actual law, or merely an order by the manager of some mine, or simply the pressure of European opinion. But that is by no means the only kind of colour bar. It is not even the most important. And in some of the countries of British East Africa, that are governed under the authority of Imperial Parliament, colour bars are as numerous and as high as in South Africa, are more fully elaborated indeed than anywhere else in the world. This book will describe how it was that colour bars came to be erected in those countries, will examine some of the laws and other measures that they consist of, and give some account of how they operate in people's lives.

It may be as well to begin by giving the outline of a typical colour bar of the more important sort. In Kenya, as in the rest of British East Africa, the Government ensures the education of all the European children in the country. Most of them go to Government schools, at a cost to the Government of over £23 per child per year, exclusive of heavy capital charges for school buildings, one of which cost over £40,000. No African child is allowed to enter the schools for European children. Of the African children in Kenya, about 1 per cent. go to Government schools, about 23 per cent. go to schools belonging to Christian Missions and the rest get no education at all. On the 1 per cent. the Government spends less than £7 per child per year. It gives grants to some of the Mission schools that amount to 12s. per child per year. And the total expenditure by Government on the education of all the African children in Kenya works out at about 4s. 3d. per child per year. The subject is dealt with fully in a later chapter. These bare figures are cited here to make clear exactly what the more important kind of colour bar is. This educational bar, like the others we shall examine, has a basis in law. European and African education are governed by different rules and regulations. We shall find that not all the discriminatory measures to be encountered ought properly to be called colour bars. But the longer term is so awkward for common use that the shorter one will often be used in these pages for any measure taken by a Government that discriminates on the ground of race.

One would expect to be able to refer to some official document, in which the reasons for adopting this policy of discrimination in East Africa were explained. One would think that somewhere authoritative directions could be found, laying down which discriminations were permissible, and in what circumstances, and which were not. But nothing of the kind exists. What makes this lack of any authoritative exposition of the policy of discrimination, or the colour bar, all the stranger, is that until about fifty years ago, all discrimination on racial or religious grounds was expressly forbidden in many expositions of Imperial policy of the most authoritative kind. To this day in fact no colour bars exist in most of the older Colonies. All we have to go on is some such vague statement as that discrimination is suited to " mixed " communities in Africa. What is meant by that is that some of the European residents in East African countries have made their homes there, which Europeans hardly ever do in West Africa. There are 65,000 of them in Southern Rhodesia, or 6 per cent. of the population. In Kenya there are 20,000 (and about 50,000 Indians) or about 0·7 per cent. of the population. In the other East African countries the proportions are smaller still. But there are other British colonies in the tropics where there are no colour bars, though the Europeans who have made their homes in them are as large a proportion of the population as in Rhodesia. Wherein lies the difference?

The educational colour bar in Kenya that we have just glanced at is clearly a case of adaptation. But adaptation to what? Is it to differences in the places in society that the children are to fill when they grow up? If it is, who determines what those places are, and on what grounds? Or is the difference in treatment due to differences, real or alleged, in the natures of the children themselves? Obviously before we can form any judgment on any single discriminatory measure, and still more before we can judge the East African policy as a whole, we must address ourselves to a range of facts that have no obvious direct connection with law and economics.

Not now, but by the time readers reach the end of this book, they will have to judge whether the measures of discrimination that we shall be examining were and are necessary. Or if not strictly necessary, then desirable. To do so, we must find the answer to the question, what in fact are the differences between the people of East

Africa and ourselves. Up to a point the answer is obvious. The people of East Africa are far poorer and more ignorant than we are—in a word, less civilized. But why are they? It is the fashion to brush such questions aside, as if whichever answer we give them could make no practical difference. We shall find, on the contrary, that no question is more pertinent to our subject than the one we have just stated. The vital question is, do history and circumstances provide the complete explanation of the fact that East Africans are less civilized than we are? Are they backward because they have had less opportunity to become civilized than we have had? The Greeks of Socrates' day called our ancestors barbarians, and so they were. They were quite as backward then as Kikuyu and Zulu are now, though their natural endowments were the same as ours. Is the reason the same in both cases? Or is there something about the minds and characters of these "natives" that is an additional explanation of their inferiority of attainment? As we proceed, we shall discover how that question has been answered by those who have been and are in authority in East Africa, not in word but in deed, in the measures that have been taken and are still in force. But let us ourselves be clear from the start as to what is at stake in the answer.

If in Africans' minds there is something lacking that we have, then they ought to be treated differently. If they are unfitted by nature for liberty, and are incapable of practising the arts of a free society, then what they need and will always need is alien government, together with a Society for the Prevention of Cruelty to Natives, like the societies that among us prevent cruelty to Children and Animals. If Africans' inferiority is in some measure inherent, it is criminal folly to allow them to be instructed in Christianity and Islam, which teach that all men, being the children of one God, are brothers. In that case the Golden Rule, that we try to follow in our behaviour to one another, would fail us. We would cease even to be kind if our inferiors claimed equality with us or tried to assert their independence. Whereas if the opposite answer to our question be the true one, so that a tribe's or a nation's inferiority of attainment is due solely to inferiority of opportunity, we must accept consequences no less clear and exigent. If Kikuyu and Zulu children have natures and capacities the same as our children have, they deserve, since they would equally profit by, the same opportunities. In that case there can be no reason why they should not govern themselves when they grow up as our children will, except the lack of the opportunities that our children have. So far asunder, accordingly, are the alternative courses of action that hang on the answer given to that question. In order to understand how it is being answered in East Africa in 1940 we must first go back some way into the past.

Just over a century ago our country had at length been roused by a long agitation to recognize the evils that had resulted from governing the colonies in the interest of the countrymen of those who governed them. Those ancestors of ours gave our question a clear and dogmatic answer and acted upon it. In the confident belief that Asiatics and Africans lacked only opportunity to become as civilized as Europeans, they applied as the cure for those evils the simple and drastic remedy of making all the inhabitants of the colonies equal before the law. At that time, of course, Governments interfered far less than now in the lives of their subjects and did far less for them. But in so far as Governments either gave or required services, complete equality was insisted on, even between the freed slaves and their former masters. Black ex-slaves served in the militia and the police, and on juries, and sent their children to the same schools as their masters' children went to, where there were any. The enforcement of the policy of equal rights for all met with fierce opposition from those masters and their influential friends at home. Rebellion was averted only by the payment by our country of £20,000,000 in compensation, not to the slaves but to their owners.

The defeat of the opponents of the policy of equal rights was believed at the time to be final. We shall find in these pages that it was not. Men who believe in and practise the policy of inequality, of discrimination on the ground of race, are in practically unchallenged authority in half of British Africa. But not, be it noted, in those colonies where the policy of equal rights was enforced a century ago, in the West Indies for example. Commission after commission has exposed the neglect that these islands have suffered under the Colonial Office, that is notably to be seen in the failure to use the large estates for peasant settlement and in the inadequate taxation of wealth. But we may get a rough idea of the results of the three different policies that our country has pursued in governing Africans by comparing the conditions that prevail in the three groups of colonies that are populated by people of African descent. In the West Indies, where the policy of equal rights has hardly been encroached upon, the daily income of an ordinary labourer is from 2s. to 4s. In British West Africa also colour bars hardly exist. But there the adoption of European standards of civilization has increasingly been discouraged by the authorities. In West Africa the labourer's daily income is, when an allowance is added for the value of home-grown food, from 9d. to 1s. 6d. In British East Africa, where the policy of the colour bar pervades all life, it is, again allowing for the value of home-grown food, from 4d. to 9d. When tested by standards of social health the same contrast appears. In Kenya and Southern Rhodesia the jail population, including those in " detention camps," is the highest in the world, except for one Baltic State. In Jamaica it was, five years ago, among the lowest in the world. We smile when told that in some West Indian Islands the birthday of every British sovereign since Queen Victoria is a public holiday. Yet so rare a sign of gratitude for rights and liberties conferred a century ago is profoundly significant.

It is important to note that colour bars are found only in British Africa. They do not exist in French, Portuguese or Belgian Africa. When a train crosses the international boundary between Northern Rhodesia and the Belgian Congo, the " white " guard and engine-driver, who are paid at least a pound a day, hand over to their " black " counterparts, who at most are paid 5s. a day.

Some people, who think it important that no British Government or statesman has ever repudiated the policy of equal rights, lay great emphasis on the distinction between statutory and administrative discriminations. They believe that so long as they are merely administrative, that is to say are not enforceable by law but are within the discretion of the competent authority, a reforming Governor could do away with colour bars without having to consult his Executive or his Legislative Council. It is quite true that, in the case just cited, the Governor of Northern Rhodesia could, if supported from Downing Street, take action by himself that would enable Africans to drive railway engines. But few colour bars can be dealt with so simply as can those that merely restrict Africans to kinds of work that are so poorly paid that Europeans do not want to engage in them. In African circumstances, in fact, colour bars that have no legal support have a natural tendency to crumble. In Kenya, for example, some Africans have recently been allowed to drive railway engines. (All railways in British Africa, with one exception, are state-owned.) Because their general education is so defective they are apt to drive carelessly. Fortunately for them, however, the doctrine of equal pay for equal work finds no favour in Africa. So employers have a strong incentive to use them.

It is hardly necessary to mention that this book will have no concern with colour bars that arise from personal conviction or prejudice. Hotel-keepers in London, for example, often refuse accommodation to coloured people. All that sort of thing is secondary, and would soon be as rare in London as it is in Paris and Lisbon if Governments took down their colour bars. There are of course border-line cases. A few years ago a man sub-let part of his township plot in Salisbury, Southern Rhodesia, to an African. Threatened with social ostracism, he retracted from the undertaking. That was a social rather than a political case. We had best confine our attention to the most important kind of colour bar, namely those that have some sort of statutory fortification. The methods that Governments use with that purpose are various. The Public Services Act of Southern Rhodesia simply excludes " native and coloured persons " from its scope. In that country no African employed by either the Government or the municipalities gets a wage that is more than a fraction of what the lowest-paid European employee gets. A few colour bars are erected by indirect means, by a measure that seems to have some quite different purpose. A case of that kind is described in Chapter IV. But the commonest way, notably in regard to taxation, education, wage contracts and labour conditions generally, is to make separate provision for Europeans and Africans by separate laws. Thus, for example, to be drunk during working hours is in Kenya a criminal offence, that is punishable by two months' imprisonment or a fine that is equivalent to a year's wages, in an African, but not in the case of a European. A complete list of the discriminatory measures in force, major and minor, would extend over many pages and would be wearisome. Also, they are not identical in all the six countries of British East Africa. In both Rhodesias and in Kenya an African's life is so beset by colour bars that the moment he leaves his village home he meets them at every turn. In Nyasaland there are perhaps rather fewer, in Tanganyika fewer still and in Uganda fewest of all, hardly any in fact.

CHAPTER II

HOW COLOUR BARS AROSE

THE facts as they are today in East Africa cannot be understood without some explanation of how they came about. The change from the policy of equal rights to the policy of the colour bar has been made, not only without any sanction by Parliament, but even without our statesmen being aware of it. So recently as after the start of the present war these men have asserted that the Empire is based on free and equal opportunity for all. Two kinds of explanation of the change are possible. It might be due to something new and different in the people of East Africa, when fifty years ago they first came under European administration, something that made the policy of equal rights harder to apply or less desirable than its application to the slaves in the West Indies sixty years earlier. That can hardly be the case. No one could assert that the people of the tribes of East Africa in 1890 were more depraved or less law-abiding or even more ignorant than the slaves were in 1834. For that matter, there are tribes in India, where there are no colour bars, that are quite as backward as any in Africa. (In India at one time a European could claim to be tried by a jury of Europeans. That sole remaining privilege was abolished many years ago.) Since nevertheless the conditions prevailing in East African society fifty years ago were held to justify and do to some extent explain the reversal of the policy of equal rights, an account of them will follow later. But as those conditions cannot be the true explanation of the change, we must look for it in the only other quarter. It must have taken place in the minds of the men who have governed in Africa, and in the mind of the nation that sent them to govern. The change was gradual. As the generation that in real penitence for past wrongs had paid a great price to get the policy of equal rights accepted died out, zeal in enforcing it died away. The mood of the country changed. The conception of what Empire meant was transformed until no longer was a country thought of as belonging to its inhabitants. Some notion of the decline in both public sentiment and official policy may be got by comparing two incidents, identical in their substance, but differing widely in their outcome.

In 1843 the New Zealand Company wanted to overturn the treaty that had been made four years before with the Maori that guaranteed them their remaining lands. The company urged that the treaty had been made with " naked savages " and that it was " merely a praiseworthy device for amusing and pacifying them for the moment." The answer ran thus: " Lord Stanley entertains a different view of the respect due to an obligation contracted by the Crown of England, and his final answer to the demands of the Company must be that he will not admit that any person or Government can contract a legal, moral or honorary obligation to despoil others of their lawful and equitable rights." Thus in 1843. Turn now to sixty years later.

Until 1903 most of what is now called the Kenya highlands was occupied by a warrior tribe, the Masai. The terror of their name had protected an immense area farther inland from slave raids, as well as from more desirable intrusion—had in fact cut it off from civilization. But as cattle raiding from other tribes and lion hunting were the sole duties of Masai youth, even the facts that a day's notice of a raid was always given and that human beings were never attacked, unless of course they tried to keep their cattle, and were never taken captive, could not save them from subjection. In 1903 both the Foreign Office, which then had charge of East African affairs, and the local Government began to give away land in the highlands to Europeans with such reckless profusion that by 1905 it was found that the Masai were left in legal possession of only patches of the central and best-watered part of their former lands. So it was decided to move the tribe right out of what is now called the Rift Valley, and to make a treaty with the Masai that would guarantee the tribe undisturbed possession " for ever " of their remaining lands. Of those lands only one area, Laikipya, has really good soil and abundant perennial water. (Most rivers and streams in Kenya run dry for a longer or shorter part of the year.) The treaty was signed in 1906. In 1911 the Governor told the Colonial Office, to which East African affairs had been transferred, that the Masai wanted to leave Laikipya for an uninhabited area elsewhere. Downing Street was not told that the reason that area was uninhabited was that it had hardly any water in the dry seasons. The Colonial Office was reluctant to agree but yielded to the assurances of the men on the spot, insisting however upon a new treaty with the tribe. As the Masai do not cultivate the soil there were no crops to be waited for. So as soon as consent was got the clans that lived on Laikipya were escorted out of it by troops with rifles. While the eviction was going on the chiefs of those clans brought an action in the court at Mombasa for the restoration of their rights under the treaty of 1906. When this bomb burst Lord Harcourt, the Secretary of State, realized that, to put it mildly, he had been misinformed, and ordered Laikipya, parts of which had already been assigned to very important people indeed, to be restored to the Masai. The Governor resigned. Lord Harcourt, however, soon went out of office and his successor gave Laikipya to the settlers after all. Some land additional to what the Government had intended to give the Masai was found for them, and in 1912 the new treaty was signed with due solemnity. But as the court to which the Masai chiefs appealed decided that the original treaty of 1906 had no legal validity, it is hard to see why the Colonial Office should have attached so much importance to the making of a new treaty.

Some of the sequels to this Masai case have as much significance as the case itself. The man whose methods of persuasion, which readers may be left to imagine, had kept the Masai chiefs quiet for so long, though not quite long enough, was rapidly promoted, and ended his career as the Governor of several important colonies. When in 1911 news of the proposal to expel the Masai from Laikipya first got about, one official wrote in protest to the Governor. A year later, when the Masai chiefs brought their action in the court, that official was expelled from Kenya for conspiring with them, though in fact he had never written or spoken to any of them. As a further lesson to others, he was kept in the lowest grade in his Department in the colony to which he was sent, until he was pensioned. Finally, in 1939, His Majesty signed two Orders in Council that deal with land in Kenya. The one proclaims the exclusive ownership by Europeans for ever of the so-called settled areas, including Laikipya. It enacts that in those areas " all native rights . . . whether such rights relate to tribal, group, family or individual holdings in any land . . . are hereby extinguished." The other Order in Council deals with " native lands." It contains clauses that empower the Governor to grant leases of such lands to Europeans, though he must consult the Land Board, no member of which is African, about the lease of any area larger than fifty acres. It is an obvious misnomer to use the term colour bar for this kind of discrimination, whereby Africans' rights in land are treated so differently from Europeans'. But there is no better term for one to use.

For many years now the Maori have sent their own representatives to the New Zealand Parliament. The reason why they do is that the men who governed the British Empire a century ago gave a clear answer to the question we began by asking, and were resolute in requiring Colonial Governors to act in accordance with that answer. They decided, that is to say, that the reason why some people in the world were naked savages was simply that history and circumstances had denied them equal opportunity with other people to become civilized, and directed those who governed them to give them that equal opportunity. The Masai are still naked savages. They are reluctant to enter the only place in modern East African society that we offer them. The reason why their fate has hitherto been so different from the Maoris' is that during the last fifty years Downing Street and Parliament and the nation have evaded that question, and have left it to be answered by men who could not be expected to give it the true answer. The Masai used to hunt lions with spears, with shields of hide the only protection of their naked bodies. Such virtue might be put to many uses in the world. But the Masai, we are told officially, are much degenerate now.

Thanks largely to the prowess of those Masai, it is only fifty years since the interior of East Africa came under the authority of British, German and Portuguese Governments. The European occupation was in the interest of the inhabitants, though their protection was not its main motive. Those inhabitants, as we shall see later, were helpless to defend themselves from freebooters of various European nationalities, whose rifles, though there was nothing for them to loot but ivory and cattle, did far more damage than Masai spears had done.

By the time East Africa was occupied, already in West Africa Africans were bank clerks and shopkeepers in towns, occupations from which in 1940 Africans are debarred in most of British East Africa. It is commonly said that the reason why British policy in East Africa is so different from British policy in West Africa is the absence in the West of the salubrious upland country, of which there is so much in the East, that is " suitable for white settlement," and hence envied and acquired by Europeans. But the soil in West Africa is richer than in East Africa. The late Lord Leverhulme was not the only man who made determined efforts to get concessions in the West. He was foiled by protests from Africans themselves that threatened the use of violent action, aided by Clifford and other Governors less pliable than most. Truer explanations of the contrast are first, that British policy in West Africa was already fixed before the decline we noted had set in, and second, that the trading posts first founded in West Africa were governed by condominiums of British traders and African chiefs. British authority, and with it the increasingly expensive machinery of government, spread slowly at much the same pace as the growth of trade and wealth. Hence the absence to this day in the Gold Coast of the direct taxation of ordinary labourers and peasants that is the dominant feature of society in British East Africa. British East Africa, by contrast, was occupied in the greatest haste, to forestall the French and Germans, and in order to prove the occupation legitimate the complete and very costly apparatus of Government was set up almost at once. So at once the question arose, in what now are the two Rhodesias, Nyasaland, Kenya and Uganda, how the cost of that apparatus was to be met. Not the sole but the main reason why British policy in East and British policy in West Africa differ is that the men who had to answer that question had conceptions of Empire very different from those their grandfathers had. Joseph Chamberlain in his old age called colonies Imperial estates, ripe for development. Cecil Rhodes recorded the hope that the map of nearly all the world would be painted red. The nation itself had travelled far since sixty years earlier it had taxed itself twenty million pounds to buy off the furiously protesting settlers of that time. What also made it hard to give a just answer to that question was that the uniquely long isolation of the region had, as will be described, left its inhabitants uniquely backward. They neither had anything to sell nor had any wish, at first, to buy what Europe had to offer. We can all see now that Britain ought to have borne the cost of governing people who had no wish to become the subjects of the Crown, until the growth of civilized ideas and habits enabled them to produce taxable wealth. What happened instead was that with one hand men were offered work, such as making roads and building stockades and houses, at two rupees or 2s. 8d. a month, and with the other hand they were each taxed two rupees. The intruding Europeans were given unquestioning obedience almost everywhere, even when this poll tax was imposed, though then it was, and now still is, regarded as proof of enslavement. It would be quite wrong to say that the Europeans' possession of rifles was what made them obeyed. What made the obedience instinctive, and what even now is the basis of European authority, is the fact that Europeans have so much greater attainments than Africans in regard to everything that we include in the term civilization. This direct taxation of all adult males in all the countries of British East Africa is one of the two measures that have created the pattern of their society. As the tax was paid practically without resistance, it was everywhere increased step by step, until in two countries bloodshed ensued; then it was somewhat reduced. The dominant place the tax holds in East African life cannot be understood apart from its background, the special character of that life itself, which will be dealt with later. A full account of the tax must therefore wait, and we shall go on to explain the other measure that has been formative of East African society.

Clearly the tax solved only part of the problem of how to meet the cost of governing. It ensured plenty of unskilled and costless labour. But it provided no money for salaries and to pay for the imported goods on which salaries are largely spent. Somehow exportable wealth had to be conjured up. It was decided to create that wealth by the only means whereby in fact it could rapidly have been created, namely by persuading owners of capital in England and South Africa to accept grants of land, and to grow on it, by employing Africans as labourers, produce for sale and export. That was done, to a greater or less extent, in every East African country. It was the other decisive step in East African history.

CHAPTER III

LAND

MOST of the land in East Africa is incapable of cultivation, and most of the rest is marginal. Vast stretches are either rainless or have a rainfall so small or so precarious that crops cannot be relied upon to ripen. Tsetse fly infests and has depopulated large areas. Other parts are covered by uneroded rock and boulders. Many areas that have enough rain are uninhabited because the soil is so poor. So the areas where soil is good and rainfall adequate are relatively quite small. Fifty years ago those areas were crowded with people—apart, that is, from the lands of the pastoral tribes (all of them small, except the Masai, of whom there are about 150,000), that live by their flocks and herds. They were crowded with people belonging to the cultivating tribes, that live by the hoe. They are even more crowded now.[1]

Clearly, in considering alienations of land to Europeans, the only areas to be taken into account are those with good soil and enough rain. Alienation was most extensive and least justifiable in the two Rhodesias. In Tanganyika,

[1] Maps can be most deceptive things. Maps of African countries should never be printed unless they show rainfall and altitude. Whether the area of Northern Rhodesia is five times or fifty times the area of England matters very little. What does matter is that the quality of its soil and the character of its climate are such that the agricultural wealth the whole country is capable of producing may quite possibly prove to be no greater than the wealth Yorkshire is capable of producing.

both the German and, since the war, the British Governments have been more careful to avoid injurious alienations. The case of Nyasaland is unique in that first Christian Missions and then traders bought land from chiefs before a British administration was set up. In Uganda, the areas that have been alienated are small and include practically no land to which any tribe could reasonably lay claim. In Kenya, though the rights of the tribes have been better respected than in the Rhodesias, they have been disregarded more than they were in Tanganyika and Uganda. Our examination of the subject will be confined to that country.

All the land in Kenya is Crown land, as is the case in most British African countries. No one, that is to say, can have any title in land except one granted by the Government. And in Kenya the Government has made grants of land only to Europeans, except for a small area granted to a score of Indian farmers in the early days. The areas that are still in native occupation, and cover about a quarter of the total area of the country, are called Reserves or Closed Areas. But in law they are simply Crown lands, the boundaries of which have been notified in the official Gazette. About 11,000 square miles have been alienated to Europeans, mostly in freehold but partly in leaseholds of 99 or 999 years. The areas alienated in part consisted of the belts of land (mainly covered with forest that now unhappily has vanished) that separated the tribes from one another. But no one would be so hardy as to deny that most of the 11,000 square miles was in native occupation at the time it was alienated. By far the biggest losers were the Masai. Their expulsion from most of and the best of their land was defended on the ground that their morals in regard to property, sex, and the taking of human life in what is called ritual murder, made it desirable that they should learn to earn their bread by the sweat of their brows, which, since forthright compulsion would raise a storm, could be done only by indirect economic pressure. Few readers will agree that the way to make bad people good is to deprive them of their land. The further reason given for the expropriation was that the Masai made such poor use of good land. So-called nomads never, of course, wander at will, but use grazing grounds in a seasonal rotation, the plains when rain has flushed the streams, the mountain sides where the springs rise when the streams below run dry. The soil in the Rift Valley is volcanic and rich. But much of it rests on pumice stone that cannot hold up water. Trees will not live on those parts, nor will any vegetation that needs water all the year. It is also deficient in certain salts and is rapidly exhausted under cultivation unless these are added. Thousands of acres in what once was Masai-land were ploughed up by their new European owners and sown to wheat. But, as happened in the Middle West for the same reasons, not only did yields rapidly fall off: soil erosion appeared. So most of the land has been left to nature again, and is being used for grazing as the Masai used it.

Between 1903 and 1920 nearly all the tribes in Kenya lost some land by alienation to Europeans. That would probably be officially admitted now. It is said in excuse that the land was taken in ignorance of native rights to it. Even if that were true, and it is not, it is hard to see how it would make the case any better. The people belonging to the cultivating tribes who lost their land in that way are called squatters. (In South Africa that word has a somewhat different meaning.) An account of the squatters is contained in the next chapter. Theirs is an exceptional case. The point to note is, not that most Africans in Kenya were dispossessed by the alienations, for that was not the case, but that there is no land available for the minority who have been dispossessed. Practically all the land in the country that is fit to cultivate and is not contained in the Reserves has already been alienated. How the area of land of that character is distributed is unknown. The writer's opinion, for what it is worth, is that there is about as much of it in the twelfth of the total area of the country that has been granted to Europeans as there is in the quarter of the total area that consists of Reserves. One would not expect the 11,000 square miles of alienated land to include much inferior land, since Europeans would not want any. However that may be, whether most of the land that deserves to be called arable is in native occupation or in European ownership, the indisputable fact is that it is all gone. The land in the huge areas of unalienated Crown land is either marginal or worthless. Conclusive proof of that statement is provided by the failure of the repeated efforts of the Government to find men who will accept free grants of land. For over thirty years the Government has done all it could to increase " white settlement." The reader is referred to the writer's second book, *A Last Chance in Kenya*, for an account of the privileges and subsidies it has devised to tempt people with capital to settle in the country. Since that book was written it gave the settlers over £200,000 in hard cash, nominally in loans to tide them over the depression. Though no one ever imagined the money would ever be repaid it was only in 1939 that

LAND

Parliament was told the debtors were no longer being asked to repay what they had been lent. Yet, despite all its efforts for a generation, the Government has failed to find applicants for the still unalienated Crown land. Already, in fact, a considerable number of estates have been abandoned and lie derelict. And it is certainly true that the great majority of the men to whom grants of less than 4,000 acres were originally made have abandoned them by this time.

This matter is so important that the facts will be recapitulated. Of the land in the country, one-twelfth belongs to Europeans and is inhabited by some 1,600 landholders, their dependants and 110,000 African employees. About half the land in Kenya that is worth cultivating lies within that one-twelfth. One-quarter of the total area is in tribal occupation, each tribe's land being called a Reserve. Most of the land in the Reserves is uninhabited. The habitable parts are intensively cultivated by about 3,000,000 Africans (when not at work for wages), have a density of 150 to 300 per square mile, and comprise the rest of the land in the country that is worth cultivating. The remaining two-thirds of the total area, the unalienated Crown land, are uninhabited and contain practically no land that is worth cultivating.

A note may be desirable on climatic conditions in East Africa. Few indeed are the places in East Africa where a harvest can be counted on as confidently as in England. Even in favoured parts droughts, floods or locusts commonly destroy the grain crop every third year or so, and the potatoes, yams and other roots that lie for years in the ground as a reserve, are eaten. Areas with too little rain for cultivation may still provide herbage for stock. But they can be so used only if there are other areas, not impracticably distant, to which stock can be sent during the dry seasons. The writer is aware that this account of the case is at variance with the reports of several land commissions. He suspects that the members of those commissions did not traverse on foot some of the areas on which they reported, at the time of year when water is hardest to get.

One-sixth of the land in the European-owned 11,000 square miles is officially reckoned to be in " beneficial occupation," though the standards used, in regard to such matters as fencing and number of acres per head of stock, are lower than in Australia and other countries. Rightly so, because of the deficiencies of the soil. The proportion of those " settled areas " that is being put to some sort of use and the number of Europeans who live in them have not appreciably increased during the last twenty years. When the first grants of land were made, conditions were attached to them with the purposes of excluding speculation, by prohibiting the sale of the land, of ensuring its early development, and of enabling the State to acquire some part of increased land values. All those safeguards were speedily abandoned. It is no exaggeration to say that since 1912 in every battle between the settlers and the Colonial Office, the representative of the public interest, the settlers have won. Why that has been the case is to the writer a complete mystery. The sums the Government received in return for grants of land were anything from a fifth to a fiftieth part of the value of the land when the grants were made. Two cases cited in the writer's first book, *Kenya*, will show the sort of thing that happened. A Mr. Hall was granted 642 acres in 1906, for which he paid the Government £171 and survey fees of £12. Then he found the surveyor had made a mistake and that he had only 582 acres. The surrounding land was all privately owned. Mr. Hall sued the Crown for the value of the missing sixty acres. The court awarded him £300 or £5 an acre, as compared with 6s. 3d. an acre that he had just paid the Government for the land. The other case was of a farm of 640 acres of specially good land near Nairobi. It was granted to A. in 1903, in return for £85. Two years later A., who had bought it for re-sale, sold the land to B. for £640. B. too meant to re-sell. But, unlike A., he had capital. He built a stone house on the estate and laid down 150 acres to coffee. He spent £5,000 altogether in eight years on improvements to the property and during that period his income from sale of produce just covered his capital expenditure. He sold the estate in 1913 for £17,000. That sort of thing happens no longer. The present owner of that same estate would probably be happy to sell it for £1,000.

The statement that probably half the land in the country that is worth cultivating is in private European ownership would be denied by the authorities. It has some support from two sources. The annual trade returns distinguish those of the goods exported from Kenya that are produced on the European plantations from all the rest of the exported goods. Of the goods exported that are not the produce of the plantations, more than half the value has, during the last three years, been represented by gold. The next largest item is hides and skins, the produce of the pastoral tribes, that live by their cattle. The value of the goods exported that are left when the value of exported gold and hides and skins is deducted will, mainly or wholly, represent the value of the produce for export of the agricultural tribes, who comprise 90 per cent. of the population. And the sum so arrived at has never in recent years amounted to as much as 4 per cent. of the total value of the goods exported. Unfortunately, though what those facts imply is quite true, namely that very few Africans in Kenya have land to spare on which to grow produce for sale, a recent development makes such an inference not strictly a fair one. During the last few years the agents of a European firm have begun to buy food crops from the peasantry just after harvest, when they are plentiful. And such of the goods thus bought as are eventually exported seem to be included, in the trade returns, in the figures of plantation-produced exports. From the information available it appears that this new trade is confined to the Kavirondo country, and also that most of the produce that is bought in times of plenty is resold to the peasantry at double the price or more in times of scarcity. No doubt in time the Kavirondo will learn the folly of such improvidence. Its importance to us lies in the fact that the trade returns no longer enable us to be certain that the 90 per cent. of the population produces no more than from 2 per cent. to 4 per cent. of the value of the crops of the country that are grown for sale. The additional sum involved in this sort of trade, the benefits of which are probably more than dubious, are sure to be small. But proof that they are is lacking.

In both Rhodesias production for sale is even more completely in European hands than in Kenya. Of the coffee and other produce that is exported from Tanganyika, on the other hand, the bulk is grown by the African peasantry. Of the goods exported from Uganda, nearly 90 per cent. is produced by Africans, most of whom, however, have to pay their chiefs a money rent for the land on which the produce is grown.

LAND

The other piece of evidence to support the statement that half, or quite possibly more, of the good land in Kenya is in European ownership is the way expenditure on roads and bridges is allocated. All trunk roads, wherever they are, are made and kept up by the Government. It also bears the whole cost of feeder roads in the " settled " areas, where the land, that is, belongs to the settlers. But feeder roads in the Reserves have to be made and kept up by the N.A.s of the tribes through which the roads pass. Until a few years ago that work was done by levies of forced and unpaid men. Since the time when the Geneva Convention prohibited the Government from using compulsion, the work has had to be paid for. Its cost is met out of the tribal rates or cesses, as also is a large part of the cost of education in tribal areas. In the " settled " areas no money is raised by local rates for either education or roads, all expenditure on roads being borne by the Government. The result is that in the Budget, where the expenditure on roads and bridges in the settled areas is shown separately from what is spent on them in the rest of the country, we find that five times as much is spent on roads and bridges in the former as is spent on them in the latter areas. In other words, the Government spends on the means of transport in that twelfth part of the country where the land belongs to Europeans five times as much as it spends in the rest of the country, including both Crown lands and Reserves. When it is borne in mind that without means of transport crops cannot be marketed, the significance of that proportion will be realized. On the same ratio, the land in the settled areas would seem to have five times the value of the land still unalienated and in the Reserves. The writer prefers his own rough estimate that the land that is of any agricultural value is about evenly divided between the settled areas and the Reserves.

Though this instance of discriminatory treatment in regard to roads cannot be called a colour bar, it shows clearly how discrimination between Europeans and Africans inevitably works out to the disadvantage of Africans.

CHAPTER IV

THE SQUATTERS

THE preamble of an Ordinance (the local name for a law) that was enacted in Kenya in 1918 runs thus: " Whereas it is desirable to encourage resident native labour on farms and to take measures for the regulation of the squatting or living of natives in places other than those appointed for them by the Government." No one reading those words would suppose that the " places other than those appointed " were simply tribal lands, the homes for generations, the only homes of thousands of Africans. In 1918 and for years afterwards that fact was officially denied. Now, however, the last N.A.D. report refers to squatters as " right-holders on private and Crown lands." But the Colonial Office was told the truth about them, namely that the men's homes had been given to Europeans, only when, in the judgment of the Government at least, it was too late for their equitable rights to be restored. We used to be told that squatting was due to the attractions of the propinquity of Europeans. There was some truth in that. Some Africans do prefer to live on European plantations. In every country there are people who correspond to the boys who run away to sea or go elsewhere to see life. Few would contemplate life for long if it meant working for 6s. a month, which is what the N.A.D. says that squatters commonly get.

The number of those " right-holders " on private land

is officially estimated to be 104,000. The number of those of them who live on Crown land is unknown. Most will be in the Forest Reserves, since, as we saw, the other areas of Crown land are practically worthless. In Forest Reserves squatters are apt to do much damage. The tribe most numerously represented among the squatters is the Kikuyu, and they happen to have unusually individualistic ideas and laws about land. There is so much diversity in the customary law of African tribes that few general statements are true of all tribes. Only two perhaps are true of all tribes. All the members of either a clan or a village have the right to use uncultivated land, that is used for grazing or as the source of firewood or wood for building or grass for thatching, or fruit or shade trees with long life. The other general rule is that rights in land are forfeited after a period of disuse that varies with the tribe and sometimes with the clan. The rights in land of cultivating individuals and families vary greatly from tribe to tribe. In many tribes, among them the Kikuyu, the land is regarded with strong emotion, as the place where the spirits of the dead live and may be approached, to whom in due time the living will be united. But the Kavirondo do not seem to have so strong a bond with the locality, probably because they are a recent amalgam of two tribes that spoke quite different languages, the larger of which came from much farther north to where both now live. The Kikuyu, however, had a system of land tenure that nearly approached individual freehold. And so, when perhaps 50,000 of them found that their homes belonged in law to the white strangers, they just stayed on. As we shall see in a later chapter, there was no room for them elsewhere. For in the Kikuyu Reserve other families and clans were as attached to their land as they were to theirs, and, even apart from other considerations, could not have spared land on which to grow food for large numbers of people of other clans. So most squatters took service with the new owners, and as they were, and are, at the disadvantage of having nowhere else to live, are commonly paid less than standard rates.

By 1918, however, a number of them had begun to rent the land that once had been their own from the owners, paying as much as 10s. an acre or more for it. The settlers objected to that development. So the Government made the law to stop the practice, the preamble of which we quoted. The one thing settlers always object to is that Africans should have a right in law the same as their own. When considering this Resident Natives' Ordinance which, variously amended, is still in force, it must be remembered that the Colonial Office, when it consented to the measure, had no idea that the great majority of the squatters had every right in equity to the land they occupied. It was told that there was plenty of room for them elsewhere in " places appointed for them by the Government."

The R.N.O. makes it a heavily punishable offence for a land-holder to accept payment by an African, in money or in kind, for the use of land. It also makes it an offence for an African to live at all anywhere outside his tribal Reserve or in townships, except on certain conditions. The chief conditions are that the Resident Native Labourer (R.N.L.) must enter into a contract of service with the owner of from one to five years: that the magistrate whose consent to the contract is necessary may give it only if he is satisfied that the owner can give the R.N.L. work: that the R.N.L. must work for the owner for at least 180 days of each year, on such days as the owner chooses:

and that on the holding that it is the owner's duty to provide the R.N.L. on which to grow his own and his family's food, he may grow only such crops as the owner permits. An amending Ordinance provides that when land is sold, the R.N.L. passes with it into the service of the new owner, until he finishes his contract. A Bill introduced into the Legislature by the Government in 1938 provided that the minimum number of days' work a R.N.L. must do should be increased to 270. But the clause making the change was dropped, presumably by direction of the Colonial Office. It may be noted that though an Ordinance enabling the Government to fix minimum wages is on the Kenya statute book, though never used, and though squatters are notoriously badly paid, the Ordinance makes the fixing of a R.N.L.'s minimum wage no part of the magistrate's duty.

This Ordinance deserves careful attention as both an illustration of new-style colonial policy and an example of a carefully designed and indirect colour bar. It does not even mention the words buy and lease. Yet none the less it effectively makes it a crime for an African either to buy or to lease land. No similar law exists in Tanganyika, Uganda or Nyasaland. But a law with the same purpose and even more restrictive provisions is in force in Southern Rhodesia.

The point that is most important of all to be grasped in studying this Ordinance is that what it prohibits is not the presence of Africans unpleasantly near their European masters. The notoriously frequent cohabitation of European men with African women alone proves that. That remark will give offence to some, and it should at once be added that European society in East Africa is vastly more respectable than it used to be. The writer will give an account of his own experience in the matter on the station in which he spent his first two years and a half in East Africa. Of about eighty English, Scots and Germans in the place, all of them at one time or another his patients, some half-dozen had their wives with them. Of the rest, about a third lived quite openly, and as a rule quite happily, with African concubines, who did their cooking and mending and often sat in the front veranda. A number of the rest were more or less furtive about it and kept the women to the back veranda. Quite a number of course had nothing to do with African women. But in all the years the author spent in Africa, he only once came across a man who attributed his abstention to natural repugnance. All that was nearer forty than thirty years ago. Though we are not concerned with social colour bars, the argument that legal equality would result in undesirable social equality must be met, the argument that often takes the form of the taunt, " Would you like your daughter to marry a black man ? " One would answer that all unions, legal or not, between persons who have widely different attainments in civilization are likely to prove unfortunate. But also, that if black and white were given equal opportunities to reach attainments, the kind of emotion that gives rise to that jibe about marrying a black man would fade away. And that even as things are now, the author would rather his daughter married one of several black men he has known than any one of many white men he has known, though if she did, her countrymen, and especially her countrywomen, would give her a hard time.

Apart altogether from this matter of sex, which however seems decisive, it should be noted that the great majority of domestic servants, in East as in South and West Africa, are " boys." Since Africans have hairless faces, they look younger than they are. Many a mistress whose " boy " wakes her every morning to give her a cup of tea would be surprised to hear that he had a wife and children at home. Grown Africans are commonly entrusted too with the sole care of European children and infants. What is objected to, and with passionate conviction, as this Ordinance illustrates, is not the nearness of Africans, but that they should enjoy civil liberties, that they should have, in their own country, equal rights with immigrant Europeans. And that objection is sustained, and, as we have seen, made valid in law, by legislation designed for that purpose by Governors chosen by Secretaries of State, to whose policies Parliament therefore has given tacit consent.

What led to the disclosure of the fact that most squatters have an equitable right to the land they occupy was that during the depression, when the price of maize and wheat hardly covered the cost of their transport to the sea, many landowners would not or could not pay squatters the money they needed to pay the tax. In these circumstances it was to the credit of the Government that it shrank from enforcing the law by evictions. When the Colonial Office learned the truth and realized the magnitude of the problem, it directed the Government to suspend the enforcement of the law until suitable Crown land was found on which to settle squatters whom landowners could not provide with work. As has already been observed, no such land exists. The largest of the areas recommended for the purpose by the last Land Commission is, to the writer's personal knowledge, incapable of supporting human life. On a journey on foot from Fort Hall to Kitui, over the old caravan route from

THE SQUATTERS

Mombasa to Uganda, that forty years ago was white with human bones, no water could be found for forty miles, though the rains were not due for two months more.

We may consider, for a moment, how squatters would fare under the policy of equal rights. First, each Reserve would be vested in the tribal authority, in trust for the tribe, exactly as land belonging to a college or hospital in England is vested. Second, squatters and other landless Africans would be as free to buy and lease land as Europeans now are. But in view of the injustice they have hitherto suffered, the Government would acknowledge the moral obligation to find free holdings for all who wanted them. Where those holdings should be, whether where the squatters now live, or on abandoned estates, or on private land resumed by the Crown for the purpose, is a question that should be decided in Kenya rather than in London, after consultation with all the parties concerned.

A recent incident well illustrates what happens as the result of alienating tribal land. Cattle in Africa are used to pay the marriage dowry and for other reasons too have more than an intrinsic value. One creditable result of British government is that agricultural tribes that formerly hardly dared keep cattle for fear of raids by pastoral tribes do now keep cattle. Their multiplication, on areas much reduced by alienation, results in that new scourge of so many countries, soil erosion. The Kamba tribe in Kenya has notably suffered from this sequence, of land alienation, unduly prolific herds, and rapidly diminishing fertility of soil : the first step in the sequence, land alienation, finds no mention in official reports. The Government dealt with this problem in the Kamba country by " de-stocking " the land section by section and reconditioning each section when bare of cattle. The firm of Liebig was induced to erect a factory for making beef extract out of the redundant cattle, which, so poor was their condition, sold for an average price of less than 30s. a head. The Kamba felt so strongly the loss of their cattle that, when protests to the local officials proved vain, over a thousand of them, men and women, walked some eighty miles to Nairobi, and sat down in the grounds of Government House, practically on the Governor's doorstep. After they had stayed there, day and night, for over a week, the Governor gave way and returned to their owners such of the cattle as had not been killed.

CHAPTER V

AS SEEN FROM THE OTHER END

SO far we have confined ourselves to East African society as it has been determined from without, by British agents in Downing Street and in Africa. And it is certainly true that Africans had no part in the devising of their taxes, and did not willingly surrender so much of their land. By this time readers may well wonder why it is that, if half of what they have so far read is true, no protest gets to us from the people themselves. That is a reasonable and pertinent question that deserves to be met.

The prime fact about the people of East Africa, that explains their state of mind and their behaviour, is that until fifty years ago they were as completely cut off from civilization as if they were living on another planet. The southern parts of the region were ravaged by slave raids during the first three-quarters of last century. In previous centuries the traffic in slaves went westward, with its operative force the avarice of Europeans, the English above all. Indeed for a time we had a monopoly of the slave trade to the Americas, wrested in war from Spain. Then, as we noted, we repented for a time, and when Arabs took the place of Europeans, and continued, from East Africa, to supply the demand for slaves by Turkey, Persia and Arabia, as well as by the United States until the civil war, and by Brazil even later, we, almost alone among the nations, gave many lives and much money to bring the trade to an end. Livingstone, who died in what now is Northern Rhodesia, predicted that the motives for enslavement would persist, and find new means of expression. He noted in his Last Journal that, until slave raids had devastated the region, spinning, weaving and other civilized arts had flourished. Farther north, even those arts were unknown to most of the tribes. Most of them lived in short in pure tribalism—some of them even had no chiefs, nor even a word meaning chief.

In matters of the mind we are as grievously at the mercy of the fashions as in what we wear. It is the fashion now to admire tribal life, even to compare it favourably with civilized life. It is quite true that since all the members of a tribe believe themselves to be both related by blood and united to the spirits of the dead and the yet unborn, they feel and behave to one another as if they were all one family. That seems wholly admirable to us. But not all families are harmonious, and in tribal as in civilized society, the strong sometimes despoiled the weak. Again, the economic problems that vex us seem to vanish when such work as building a hut or house is done by the whole village, without payment, except for a feast of meat and beer, and dancing to follow. Food, too, was shared, so long as there was any. Thirty years ago people in East Africa could not be got to believe that a country existed where some starved and others had more than they could eat. Among themselves, savages are in general gentler in their manners than the civilized and they are punctilious to a fault. But on nearer acquaintance tribal solidarity takes on a different guise. As a man of another tribe was outside the family circle he might be killed or left to starve. Witchcraft and other superstitions caused endless cruelty. Tradition was all-powerful and regulated all life. It is not that traditions are changeless, though the people believe they are. Their one virtue indeed is their elasticity, the way they at once adapt themselves to change in people's minds and habits. For example, fifty years ago land, among the Kikuyu, was never sold. If a clan dwindled it would adopt children from some other clan that had grown too large for the land it had. But now, any young Kikuyu will tell you, not that by Kikuyu law land has become a vendible commodity, which is the case, but that it was bought and sold from time immemorial. What tradition does is to make people act in involuntary unison at any given time. Membership of a tribe was as involuntary during life as at birth. So also was the unconscious obedience to what tradition prescribed in minute detail in everything. A little girl must do her hair in the right way : after puberty it must be done in another style : when a bride in yet another : when a mother in still another : when past child-bearing neglect is the fashion. This involuntary obedience to rules gives a tribe the character of a hive of bees rather than of a fraternity. At close quarters, the instinctive uniformity, as of the blades of grass in a field, seems repulsively inhuman. (The solidarity the Nazis are trying to create in Germany, as well as their xenophobia, are essentially an attempt to revive tribal ideas and practice.) In a civilized society it takes all sorts to make a world : in a tribe it takes only one sort. Heresy is crime and contumacy in disobeying established practice is punished by exile if not by death. (There is a small tribe in Kenya that in part at least is descended from such exiles, most of them couples who preferred one another to the partners their parents had chosen for them and been paid for. By this time the tribe has elaborated a rigid code of its own.) Everybody must agree about everything. A tribal court will spend days arguing over a trifle, but must, in the end, come to a unanimous decision.

The converse of this unanimity, this one-mindedness of the many, is that the individual's power to think and act for himself atrophies from disuse. As payment for personal work was unknown, so were individual enterprise and initiative. Hence the lack in men reared in tribalism of those virtues that Capitalism has taught the reluctant workers of Western Europe, veracity, honesty about money, and, above all, reliability. Uncivilized man is never reliable and is incapable of pursuing for himself impersonal ends. (A friend with much longer experience than the writer's in East Africa strongly dissents from that verdict. He says some uncivilized people are reliable.) In tribal society, also, to give an answer that is known or suspected to be unwelcome to the questioner is not only bad manners. It is also morally wrong. (In many cases the two concepts are indistinguishable.) If the answer given happens to be a lie, that is nothing, so long as no disagreeable result ensues. So the features of tribal life that so attract us, the absence of prisons, prostitutes, social grades, political parties, religious sects, are really evidence of underdevelopment. People who are reared in tribes have not eaten of the tree of knowledge that bears much evil fruit as well as good. They are the slaves of ideas and habits of their own unwitting creation.

All that was true of life in most East African tribes fifty

years ago. It is partly true still. How true depends on the degree to which a tribe has been exposed to the discordant and sometimes conflicting influences that we have introduced. Courts now, for example, give majority decisions. Some observers exaggerate the extent of the changes, others shut their eyes to them. Several inferences stand out clearly from the account of tribal life just given. One is that the tribal inheritance positively unfits men for modern industry. Life in a tribe treads patiently the daily round, changing only with the seasons of the revolving year, each man sustained in every act by the example of his fellows. People protect one another like trees in a forest. Modern industry demands the qualities that a tree buffeted on a hilltop acquires. That is why East Africans to-day are in much worse case than their cousins the slaves, who a century ago were given equal rights with their former masters. Morally, the tribesman is by far the better man. Even some of his virtues are a handicap to him, such as his generosity, until he finds how dangerous it is in civilized life.

Another clear inference is that people so ill-prepared for modern industry need protective legislation far more than European workers do. They do not get it. Compensation for accidents, sick pay, pensions, all are lacking. The authorities have the audacity to say that all such services may safely be left to mutual aid in the Reserves. Though the Kenya N.A.D. reports that men sometimes work for nothing but their food, the Government has never once used the machinery it has for fixing minimum wages.

A third inference is that East Africans now, many of them only one generation removed from undisturbed tribalism, must be very inefficient workers. They are.

Even we abuse new knowledge. We have turned the discovery how to fly into the means of mass destruction. Small wonder that Africans have, let us say, an inadequate appreciation of the uses to which money may be put. The settlers would put it much stronger than that. Indeed they have a real case against those modern anthropologists who teach, not as Tylor and Frazer taught, that Africans are leaving the stage of society that our ancestors left centuries ago, but that they have developed a different " culture " from ours, and are travelling a different road, with different stages. At what stage of African culture, one wonders, is individual responsibility reached ? Quite apart from the fact that there is no custom or feature of African life that cannot be matched in some other continent, the hardest of all the hard facts of contemporary East African society is that henceforth Africans must travel our road. Already now they must obey our laws. Already now, as we shall see later, they are enlisted into our industries and must use the same machines as those our workers use. In their present state of half-emergence from tribal life, driven blindly and dumbly into the society that their lords and masters so mismanage, and held back in that society by colour bars, they are, as fellow travellers, not merely exasperating but maddening. Let the reader put himself in the place of a settler, working desperately to avoid insolvency, wrestling in blistering heat with infertile soil. He must go to Nairobi and leaves his most trusted " boy " in charge of an expensive machine. He returns to find it ruined, and with it his own future, through sheer carelessness or indifference. What is the use of reminding a man in such a case that his " boy " believes him rich beyond imagining, since whenever he wants money, all he does is to write something on a piece of paper and send it to the bank ?

One can easily understand how officials and employers come to regard people as their inferiors to whom they never speak except to give them orders. (Up-country Swahili has no conjugations except the infinitive, used as a verbal noun, and the imperative.) But it is impossible for people who have never lived in Africa to realize how irresistible the conviction that Africans are inherently inferior comes to be in the minds of all Europeans except some, not all, Christian missionaries. After all, if people behave as your inferiors you treat them as your inferiors, and in the long run your beliefs correspond with your actions. In fact it is almost impossible in Africa to treat Africans as equals, except in some Mission stations, and some colleges like Achimota in the Gold Coast that are staffed mainly by ex-missionaries. What in East Africa has so overwhelming an effect on one's mind is not merely the hourly evidence of inferiority of attainment, nor even so much the universal ignorance and poverty (except for a minority of whom more later), as the universal obedience and frequent servility, that make the question whether Africans have natures and capacities the same as our own seem absurd and academic. (The writer found the grandchildren of the slaves in Jamaica anything but servile. They are exceedingly frank and friendly to strangers from England and, proud of being British citizens, look down on even white Americans. And in West Africa he found people aloof rather than servile, when they were not friendly.) Readers who behave quite naturally to Africans in London as ordinary human beings should realize that in Africa they could not, except in places that are created by people with exceptional knowledge and exceptional characters. More than that. Most readers would, after sharing for a time in the life that settlers lead, agree with them that Africans are not our equals in their natures and capacities.

And yet the sober fact is that they are. What makes that fact incredible in Africa is that there one cannot escape from the master-servant relationship. The very air in South and East Africa is so charged with the passionate conviction that black must serve white eternally that it is only when one gets clear of it that one can face the facts objectively. And that is why the men on the spot, given no national policy to pursue that is based on an objective examination of the facts, answer wrongly the vital question whether Africans' inferiority of attainment is due wholly to inferiority of opportunity, or is due also to inherent defect, and act on that wrong answer.

Between individuals in the same tribe there naturally are differences of endowment as great as between people in any village or street in England. But, judged in the mass, and provided one can exclude the effects, both in oneself and in Africans, of the semi-slavery that in South and East Africa distorts every mind, one is faced by the plain fact that no evidence exists even to suggest that Africans' minds differ from Europeans'. Some positive evidence on the matter can be found in the writer's two earlier books. What leaves the question in no real doubt is the evidence provided by history and anthropology. History displays a process of social development that is common to all mankind. It proceeds everywhere through the same stages, though not without retrogressions, so that in every continent men once lived in tribes, trembled under priests, made to themselves kings and oligarchies to obey. And this identity of the stuff of which the human mind everywhere is made is seen even more plainly in the facts revealed by anthropology. These facts show, that at the same stage of social development, men evolve the same institutions, acquire the same ideas and beliefs, and follow the same practices, in every age and in every continent.

The trouble is that objective and impersonal facts seem to men on the spot in Africa as irrelevant and as improbable as the allegation that Mars is inhabited by disembodied spirits. What the authorities profess to have done in African countries where there is a "mixed" society is simply to have made that provision for Africans which their experience has taught them to believe is fitting for them. Colour bars merely regularize and stabilize the situation. As machines were unknown in African society, no injustice can arise if the operation of some of them is reserved to Europeans. As Africans had never invented for themselves signs to indicate sounds, they have done nothing to deserve the primers we let them use, and should be grateful for the crumbs of knowledge that fall from their masters' tables. People who take that point of view, and some of them sit in high places, conveniently ignore the fact that machines, and the alphabet and the thousand other ingredients of civilization, were none of their inventing. They are a heritage, and belong of right to all mankind. Africans therefore have the same right to them as we have, if, but only if, the answer given in these pages to our vital question is the true one, if, that is to say, they can absorb that heritage and enrich their lives with it. And so long as they are denied the opportunity of doing so, no one has the right to say that they cannot. The vast contrast between what people suppose is being done in Africa, and what is in fact being done, and the resulting hypocrisy of which we as a nation are guilty, are due to our refusal to take seriously that vital question. Only if as a nation we on the one hand answer that question objectively and dispassionately, and if on the other hand we try to understand how our failure to do so during the last fifty years has left British agents in Africa exposed to the influence of those whose answer to that question is based on passionate self-interest, can good intention be translated into right policy in action. For example, European employers in Africa do honestly believe that it is the moral duty of Africans to work for them. There is nothing in that, of course. But when we find Governors echoing that view, is it not plain that they have allowed their minds to drift into the assumption that Africans are sub-human? The only way to prevent British agents from drifting into that assumption is for the nation to come to a clearly defined policy and to require those who govern in its name to act resolutely upon it.

The same assumption is at the bottom of the horror the authorities feel about " Europeanizing " or " detribalizing "—the blackest charge a man can be accused of in British Africa. If Africans are ordinary human beings, is it not natural that they should learn from Europe all and more than all that we have learned from Judæa, Athens and Rome? This doctrine, that since Africans so recently knew of no other way of life than the tribal, therefore they should not adopt any other way of life, only needs to be set down to be seen for what it is. It would mark them indelibly as sub-human, beings who cannot be prevented from watching, but may never share in mankind's slow and stumbling advance. Nothing better explains how British Africa is governed than the fact that such phrases as that " Africans should be good Africans not bad Europeans " are expected from all good Administrators. Promotion depends on a man's profession and practice of this orthodoxy. We are told that Africans are mere imitators. No one has ever tried to teach without learning that when children learn by rote the fault lies in the teaching. In any case, is not imitators just what we all are, and ought to be ? Which of us has himself created any of the things in life we most admire, value and enjoy ?

CHAPTER VI

HOW THE PEOPLE LIVE

IN fortunate countries social change is slow and all of a piece. The way their inhabitants are governed, how they provide themselves with their material needs, and what they believe about the non-sensuous world, all change together, because the essential change takes place inside the people's minds. That is not how people's lives are changing in East Africa, since there change is the result of external forces. It is true that the British agents who have had authority over East Africans made only one deliberate change in their lives. They introduced a new way of producing wealth, and induced from 30 per cent. to 90 per cent. of the men in the various countries of the region to engage in that new way. They made no concomitant efforts to change the other phases of East African life. Indeed they tried to prevent any concomitant changes. We shall deal later with the political results of the attempt to introduce an industrial revolution and yet leave the rest of life to go on as before. Its economic result has been to make people live double lives. Most of them spend two-thirds of the year in what in their eyes is the normal way at home, subtly changed though it is. But it looks much the same and it feels much the same. The other third of the year they spend in our money economy, at work for wages.

Fifty years ago, most East African tribes were ignorant

of how to spin and weave, and how to use wheels for transport and making pottery. Smelters of and workers in iron (and copper in the south) were the only craftsmen. Every family grew its own food. As differences of soil, altitude and rainfall made holdings suitable, some for certain kinds of food, and others for other kinds, the various kinds were bartered at periodical markets. It is most important to realize that almost everywhere this purely subsistence economy persists, though here and there beginning to crumble. Even in West Africa the great majority of families grow their own food, the only considerable exception being the cocoa farmers of the Gold Coast, whose industry, significantly, is not capitalistically organized. In most of East Africa every family without exception grows its own food, and over the whole region the proportion of those who do must be more than 95 per cent. So normally food is never turned into money. (In the last few years the money economy seems to have begun to spread into village life in some tribes.) So too it has come about that in East Africa, not only the growing of food, but all the other things that have to be done in people's village homes, building huts for instance, are never called work, either in English or in African languages. The word work is used only for what is done for money, in our economy that is still regarded as an artificial addition superimposed on the traditional African economy, since money itself, and the way to get it, that is earning wages, are both novelties that we introduced into African life. Europeans, curiously enough, though they give the word work, and its African equivalents, the same restricted meaning as Africans give it, take just the opposite view of the situation. " Work " in their eyes is the normal way in which Africans ought to spend their lives, and the fact that they must spend two-thirds of every year in the way they used to spend the whole of it, in supporting themselves and their families, is generally ignored and by many thought of as a sort of holiday-making.[1]

The restricted sense that the word is given locally has had important consequences. We shall soon be quoting figures relating to family incomes from official reports. But since in reckoning incomes nothing is included but money and what, being bought and sold, can be stated in terms of money, incomes so estimated are not real total incomes. The food that is grown in the Reserves and all the other work that has to be done in them have real value, even though no money value is ever put on them. So, if we take as roughly correct for East Africa the official Kenya estimate that on the average men spend two-fifths of the year earning money and the other three-fifths at home, we may say that a man's real income is in the proportion of five to two to his money income. Another result of the word's restricted meaning is that when some Governor tells D.O.s and chiefs to encourage their people to work, the Colonial Office supposes him to be merely guilty of uttering a platitude. But what in fact people are told is to go and work for wages. Another point must be explained. Most men in Kenya, as in East Africa generally, work on contract. The common contract is

[1] In August 1940 Mr. George Hall, M.P., in answering a question by Mr. Creech Jones, M.P., in Parliament, said of men who, being unable to find work in their own country of Nyasaland, go so far afield as the Rand to find it, that " the worker normally remains at work for about twelve months and then returns home to rest." An Under-Secretary of State must, of course, believe what the men in responsible positions in Africa tell him. But where else than in Africa would men in such positions describe the tasks of growing the family's food, repairing house, fences, roads, and doing all the other jobs that a small-holding demands, as " resting " ?

not for so many calendar months but for so many consecutive periods of thirty working days, oftenest six. In reckoning a working month, Sundays are not counted, nor are days not actually spent at work, whatever the cause, sickness, torrential rain making outdoor work impossible, or any other. So a six-months' contract really means seven or eight calendar months. Again, when the average labourer is estimated to spend, on an average, two-fifths of the year at work, the word average must be understood to cover, on the one hand the exceptional cases of men working for wages all the year round, and on the other the cases, also exceptional, of men who spend the whole year at home, and pay their taxes out of money saved from the previous year's earnings, or borrowed from or repaid by others.

We noted in the preface the lack of vital statistics in East Africa, and that nevertheless we would have to accept official estimates as roughly correct. But there is one exception. The number of men given in the Kenya N.A.D. reports as fully capable of work is 500,000. On the face of it, it is suspiciously round. But also, it represents a higher proportion of the total population than the number of men known to be fully capable of work in civilized countries, in which the standard of health is far higher than in Kenya, where debilitating epidemic and endemic diseases abound.

The tax is the dominant fact of East African life. It is the one and only unavoidable item in every family budget. Tax defaulters, who in Kenya number about three thousand a year, are sentenced to a month's labour in a "detention camp." The nominal incidence of the tax varies from country to country and to some extent from district to district. Some countries have a poll tax, others a hut tax, Kenya has both. In any given district in a country with a poll tax, that is to say, every male of eighteen (as a rule) and over, must pay the same sum. And in a country with a hut tax, each hut in any given district, whether owned by man or woman, is taxed the same sum. In Tanganyika and Uganda the hut tax is really a household tax, since separate huts are not taxed. In those two countries, therefore, the nominal rate is also the real rate. In Kenya it is not the real rate, since, as will be explained later, the tax is multiple. The nominal incidence of the tax is highest, 20s., in Southern Rhodesia, and lowest, 5s., in parts of Nyasaland. Clearly no general account of the tax in all the six countries of British East Africa would be accurate for any one of them. So we shall confine ourselves to the facts as they are in Kenya.

These facts, unfortunately, cannot be rightly appraised unless they are understood in some detail. And they must be seen in close relation with the facts relating both to wage-rates and to land. You cannot tell how heavy an impost is upon a man unless you also know his income. The incomes of Kenya Africans are almost wholly derived from wages. The reason for that will appear in the facts that relate to their holdings of land, which it will be convenient to examine first.

Some ten years ago two official reports were published, the one on everything to do with land among the Kikuyu group of tribes, the other on land among the Kavirondo. The Kikuyu, who live on the slopes and foothills of Mount Kenya in the highlands, are rather more than a third of the population of the country. The Kavirondo, who inhabit most of the country between the highlands and Lake Victoria, number rather less than a third.

HOW THE PEOPLE LIVE

We may take it that what is true of both those groups of tribes is also true of the smaller agricultural tribes in the country. The Kikuyu report shows that 85 per cent. of their family holdings are of from two to five acres. It also shows that the 15 per cent. of the holdings of a larger size are either high up on the mountain, or on the edge of the plain below. In the former, the ground is so steep, the cold so great, and the rain so excessive, that they produce only root crops, firewood and grass for thatching. In the latter, the rainfall is so scanty and uncertain that harvests are uncertain too. One sees many abandoned holdings on the edge of the plains, as well as new cultivation by people who, since the soil is rich, take the gamble of having either a bumper crop or no crop at all through drought.

Holdings of from two to five acres of really good land are typical of the old economy all over Africa. Readers with even the smallest knowledge of agriculture will not need to be told that they are purely subsistence holdings, especially when it is remembered that about a third of each holding must always lie fallow from lack of fertilizers. (One does not often see land lying fallow in England, as it had to in former times, because soil fertility is preserved by crop rotation and added to by manures, natural and artificial. Even now in England, however, much land needs resting for a period.) The reason why these family holdings were and are closely packed together was that crops even more than the people themselves needed protection from wild pigs, elephants, baboons and other wild animals. As these wild animals found cover in undisturbed bush, none of it was allowed to exist. Any area in East Africa that is occupied by a typical agricultural tribe consists almost entirely of small family holdings, together with such commonage as is needed for grazing, fuel and shade trees.

The Kavirondo report is less full and precise than the Kikuyu but makes it clear that the great majority of Kavirondo holdings are no larger than the Kikuyu. But that tribe has been specially fortunate. It lost little land by alienation. And its Reserve includes considerable areas of good land that are still unused. No other Reserve does. Some migration is going on from the more crowded parts to those areas, though they are remote from the railway and have no roads. In one important respect both the Kikuyu and the Kavirondo live differently from how many tribes live. Probably most of the inhabitants of tropical Africa do live as they do, crowded together on good land. But the great bulk of the total area of tropical Africa has inferior soil, and, where cultivated at all, is inhabited by tribes who must practise "shifting cultivation," clearing new ground every few years, as the soil becomes exhausted. Wherever, indeed, you find family holdings of more than five acres, you may be sure that the land is less eligible than in the smaller holdings. So the picture we should have in mind of the typical African economy is like a patchwork quilt. The patches, the ancestral family holdings, will be of various shapes and sizes, since many of them, as once was the case in Europe, consist of separate pieces or strips, some no larger than an ordinary room.

Besides the pastoral tribes, none of them of any size except the Masai, there are three minorities that do not fit into that picture. There are the squatters, whose case we have considered already. Then there are some people in every tribe, though very few except among the

HOW THE PEOPLE LIVE

Kavirondo, who are so fortunate as to be able to cultivate land in excess of their need for food. Their number cannot even be guessed at. But as the area a tribe formerly occupied included no land that was intended for any other purpose than subsistence, and as all the tribes have lost some land by its alienation, the number of families with land to spare from growing food cannot in the nature of things be large. Finally there are the people whom either economic pressure or personal preference has induced to abandon their tribal homes and to become semi-skilled workmen for Europeans. Again it is impossible even to guess what proportion of the 210,000 men who, on any given date, are at work for wages, belong to this minority. Many of course do not know themselves whether or not they will ever return to life in their Reserves. Many of them forget that if they abandon their tribal holdings for too long they lose their right in them, and will have nowhere to go when past work.

In the circumstances that have been described in the last few pages it is obvious that if most people were to be able to grow produce for sale, whereby to get money to pay the tax, they must be able to get land in addition to the two to five acres that suffice only for the family food supply. And clearly they could get additional land only from the Government, that might either have enlarged the tribal boundaries or allowed people to get land on individual tenure outside the tribal areas. Never once has the Government done either. If the contents of Chapter IV do not convince, readers should consult Mr. Ross's *Kenya from Within*, or the author's two earlier books for evidence of the fact that every Governor since Sir James Hayes-Sadler left the country has instead taken every measure short of direct compulsion to make men leave home to work for wages. That explains why the N.A.D. reports that no increase in the labour supply can be hoped for, since already 90 per cent. (which may in fact be 98 per cent.) of the men available are at work for wages for, on an average, two-fifths of the year. An unknown proportion of that 90 per cent. (or 98 per cent.) would offer themselves for employment if there were no direct taxation, or if they could get the extra land. But so long as the Government deliberately makes it impossible for them to get that extra land, as we have seen it does, wage-earning will be unavoidable for that 90 per cent. It is intended to be unavoidable.

So much for the situation of the ordinary Kenya African as regards land. The N.A.D. gives 8s. and 12s. as the upper and lower limit of standard wage-rates, for the thirty-day period already explained, for men engaged in agriculture, who number rather more than half the total number employed. Of the rest, gold miners' wages average 10s. 7d. Railway workers get rather more. And a considerable minority of clerks, school-teachers and semi-skilled artisans get much more. Kenya is the Mecca of wealthy sportsmen from all over the world. Their African valets, cooks and gun-bearers get most of all. We shall not, accordingly, be far out if we take the upper limit for the majority, 12s., as the all-round average, though no estimate of that all-round average is given by the N.A.D. The average period of two-fifths of the year spent at work is equivalent to four thirty-day working periods. That gives us 48s. as the average income from wages of the average able-bodied African male in Kenya. To that something must be added to represent the value of the hides, etc., that a minority are able to produce and sell, apart that is from foodstuffs, etc., that are grown for consumption or bartered. We saw that that sum cannot be large. If we reckon it as 12s. we shall overestimate it. So we reach £3 as the average annual money income of the average family in Kenya. And the corresponding real income will be about £7 10s. It must of course always be remembered that the majority get a good deal less than £3, and a minority much more than that sum.

We are now in a position to examine the direct taxation that Africans in Kenya have to pay. We have seen why it is that nearly all of them can get the money wherewith to pay the tax only by earning wages, and we have also seen what are the wages they get. What then do men whose land is restricted to ancestral holdings that suffice only for food, and whose money incomes average £3, and real incomes £7 10s., have to pay to their Government? The nominal rate of the Kenya hut and poll tax is 12s. (The Masai have to pay more, and in one or two small districts where both the soil and the people are specially poor the rate is less.) But 12s. is not the real incidence of the tax, since it is both a poll tax and a hut tax. If, that is to say, two lads sleep in one hut, both have to pay the 12s. But if, also, one man has more than one hut, he has to pay 12s. on each of them. Houses in the European style are increasingly being built by the best-paid small minority. But 98 per cent. or 99 per cent. of East Africans still sleep in huts, that are largish, round, windowless rooms, ventilated by eaves that overhang the walls. Africans do not live in huts but only sleep in them—do not even always use them for preparing and cooking food. So, naturally, the number of huts, or rooms, a man has depends on the number of his dependants. A widowed mother will want one for herself, for instance. Or a man may have one hut where he works and another in his Reserve. It thus comes about that some men have to pay two, four or even six taxes. Clearly the only way of getting at the real incidence of the tax is to divide its yield by the number of men in the country who are capable of work. (Women in East Africa nowadays have to do more work than they used to do, in the absence of their husbands at work for wages. They must also do kinds of work that formerly were done only by men. Some women and children do earn small sums in the tea plantations, but their aggregate amount is negligible.) As we saw, the official estimate of the number of such men is too high. But if we accept that estimate of 500,000, and divide the yield of the tax, £605,000 (tax proper £530,000 and over £70,000 of subsidiary direct taxation), by that figure, we get the sum of 24s. as the true average incidence. If, as the writer believes, the number of men who on any given date are fully capable of work is no more than 400,000, the average incidence is 30s. Personal enquiry by two friends of the author's supports the opinion that 30s., or two and a half taxes, is more likely than 24s., or two taxes, to be the true average incidence. We can now correlate the average sum paid in direct taxation with the average income, and so reveal the outline of African family economy in Kenya. Out of a money income of £3, the average family pays the Government 24s., if there are half a million men fully capable of work at one time, which is more than a third of its money income. And if, as the writer believes, the average number of men available is 400,000, the average incidence of the tax is 30s., or half the average family income. And it should be noted that though about half the taxpayers have money incomes of £2 or less, and perhaps a tenth of them incomes of £10 or more, the incidence of the tax varies, not with the size of a man's income, but with the number of his dependants.

In Southern Rhodesia incomes are higher, and in Nyasaland and most of Northern Rhodesia they are lower than in Kenya. But in all four countries the tax bears much the same proportion to the average income. In Tanganyika and Uganda the proportion is much less, since the tax is single, not multiple, and also because in Tanganyika more than half the money to pay the tax comes from the sale of native-grown produce, and in Uganda five-sixths of it is so obtained. In Tanganyika the collection of the tax in most districts is the duty of the N.A. In Kenya it is collected by the D.O.s. Its collection, in a populous district, is both arduous and distasteful. For the D.O. must combine in one person, and often perform in one day, the functions of assessing the tax, collecting and giving receipts for it, and judging as magistrate which out of perhaps hundreds of claimants to be exempted should be given exemption, and which convicted as tax defaulters. The law in Kenya permits exemptions, not, of course, on the ground of poverty, but on the ground of age, chronic disease or other permanent disability. What makes a man liable to pay the tax is simply that either he has a poll, or head on his shoulders, or he has a hut, or place to sleep in. The proportion of exemptions to assessments given in different districts varies from 3 per cent. to 30 per cent. Which of the possible reasons for so wide a variation is the true reason each reader must judge for himself. It should also be noted that, under this fiscal system, the Africans employed to count the huts are under the constant temptation to take bribes from people who want to evade the tax.

Space permits only the briefest account of the cess or

local rate. It is simply an extra tax that is levied on the same people as pay the main tax, except that huts belonging to women are exempt. The rate varies from tribe to tribe. The total amount so raised is more than £70,000. The N.A., directed by the D.O., decides how the money is to be spent. Roads and education are the largest items of expenditure. The expenditure on roads has already been dealt with. As will be noted in the chapter on education, the Government has withdrawn the subsidies it used to give the " elementary " schools, beyond which only 4 per cent. of the African children ever pass, and has thus left their whole cost to be borne out of Mission funds, out of parents' fees, and out of these local rates.

The case of the peasants in Nyasaland whose livelihood is the growing and curing of tobacco shows, however, that merely to ensure that people in East Africa can have rent-free land on which to grow crops for sale is not in itself enough to make them prosperous. In the circumstances in which they find themselves Africans hate to be regulated. What they want more than all else is to be free. Governments, on the contrary, take delight in regulating and organizing. And it should be recognized that the very nature of African staples makes most desirable some State control of industry. Manufacturers of raw materials demand uniformity of quality. So the tobacco industry in Nyasaland, like the cotton industry in Uganda, is organized and controlled by the State. In all such cases the question is, in whose interest is control by the Government exercised?

Tobacco is by far the most important industry in Nyasaland. It is a complete statutory monopoly. The law ordains that no one may plant, buy, sell or cure tobacco save by leave of the Tobacco Board, and that all tobacco must be sold over a single "auction floor," that belongs to the Board. Of the members of the Board, the majority are chosen by the Governor from among the Europeans engaged in the industry. The rest are officials. None is African. When, in 1938, the Anglo-American trade discussions were going on, Nyasaland was concerned in case the preferential duty Britain gives to tobacco that is grown in the Empire might be abandoned, in order to please the American tobacco interest. The Governor appointed a committee to report on the matter. The report was published in March 1938 and contained the following estimates:

Persons employed in the industry and deriving their livelihood therefrom:

Europeans, including growers, supervisors, buyers, transporters, graders and packers, etc.	240
Natives, growers on Native Trust Lands and private estates, 90,000; labourers, 30,000 ..	120,000

Incomes derived from the tobacco industry:

(1) European-grown tobacco, Europeans	£44,530
Natives	£35,150
(2) Native-grown tobacco, Europeans	£96,000
Transport	£48,000
Native growers and labourers:	£163,000
(3) Bank charges, interest, etc.	£6,000
(4) Profit accruing from sales abroad, returned to and circulated in Nyasaland	£46,875
Total ..	£439,555

"This figure represents the internal value of the tobacco industry and the spending power created by it."

If readers will do a little arithmetic, they will find that the average income from the industry of the 240 Europeans works out at £584—and nearly £200 a head more if "profit from sales abroad" is properly to be included. And that the average income of the 120,000 whose "livelihood" is derived from the industry is exactly thirty-three shillings. The writer did his best to get those figures verified and elucidated but failed. They are eloquent enough as they stand, but one comment may be allowed. The two high officials who signed the report were clearly quite unaware how dreadful their disclosures were.

The detailed facts that we have studied about land, incomes and taxation enable an answer to be given to the question how far compulsion to work for private employers exists in East Africa. Ten years ago thousands of men from the extreme south of Tanganyika walked 600 miles every year to plantations in the extreme north of the country to earn their tax money, though they had only a reduced tax to pay. The journey took six weeks and caused much hardship. The men went home again after an absence of about two years, laden with trade goods as well as with their own and their relatives' tax money. Information is lacking as to how far that particular migration persists. There is certainly a considerable seasonal migration from Tanganyika to Kenya. But it does seem to be the case that most people in Tanganyika can and do earn their tax money without having to leave home to work. In Uganda practically every family can support itself on land of which the tenure is secure, although, since in the early days land was vested in the chiefs, cultivators have to pay rent for their holdings.

But in Kenya and both Rhodesias people are in quite a different situation. As their Governments have deliberately made their acquisition of land impossible, have even made it a crime, what else can Africans in those countries do but accept whatever wages are offered? All manner of excuses used to be made when compulsion to work for Government was resorted to, and lofty principles were appealed to about the vast difference between making men serve their country and making them subserve private profits. When used by the authorities on the spot, such arguments were deliberately intended to deceive. The men in the Colonial Office who used them had been given proof, privately, in 1919, by the author, that they were fraudulent. And it is now sixteen years since he gave the public the truth of the matter in his first book. Fraudulent, since obviously the Government cannot provide work for all the 90 per cent. in Kenya who must find the tax money by earning wages. And when they must leave home to work for wages, what possible difference to them can it make whether their employer is a private landowner or a public Department? Presumably the reason people in this country fail to see through the fraud is that they see nothing very strange in the fact that nearly everybody in a country has to work for wages, even if, only forty years ago, no one in that country had ever done so. What people fail to see is the vast difference between wage-earning in a free country and wage-earning in a country where the workers have no votes and are too ignorant to use them if they had them : where the Government makes common cause with employers to fix wages at the level at which we have found they are : where a law designed for the purpose restricts the worker to subsistence holdings : and where, by refusing to employ men except under contract, and by making breach of contract a criminal offence, the Government makes impossible any concerted effort by the workers to raise wages or improve their condition. In a country where the workers are the majority of the electorate, and where the electorate is all-powerful, it is sheer nonsense to talk about wage-slavery. But what less ugly word have we to use to describe the cumulative effect of the colour bars we have already examined? Perhaps the clearest illustration of the essence of the case is the story of coffee in Kenya. Coffee is the most valuable and important crop in that country, and may, quite rightly, be grown only under licence. Until 1931 licences to grow coffee were refused to Africans, an instance of a purely administrative colour bar. In that year the Secretary of State published as a White Paper the dispatch he had sent to the Governors of all African Dependencies. In face of the facts it is an extraordinary document. It was written on the assumption that colour bars are things to be guarded against. But no one reading it would imagine that even one colour bar existed. It nowhere expressly prohibits all discrimination, as every similar statement of Imperial policy did until fifty years ago. But one of the few downright passages it contains runs thus: " The natives must be allowed . . . to grow such crops . . . as they think most profitable." When the matter came before the Legislative Council in Nairobi, the representatives of the settlers proposed to preserve their monopoly, and still comply with the direction of the White Paper, by raising the cost of a licence to £10, but were told by the Governor that the Colonial Office would disallow the proposal. In the end it was agreed to allow a certain number of Africans to grow coffee on "experimental plots." That was done. Some hundreds of such plots actually exist. So that one can no longer state baldly that Africans are prohibited from growing coffee in Kenya. What one can say is, however, that if any coffee is produced on those plots and sold, the amount is so inconsiderable that it finds no mention in the reports from D.O.s, that are printed in the N.A.D. report, and contain full accounts of the crops that are grown in the Reserves.

This may be the best place to deal with a common misconception. We often hear it said that Asiatics and Africans have a lower standard of living than we have. If what is meant is that they get less, the statement is quite true. But if what is meant is that they need less, then the statement is almost completely false. Almost, for two reasons. No resident in the tropics, however much or little pigment he may have in his skin, needs to spend money on keeping warm, on fuel, carpets and so on. And second, the tropic sun does seem to enable black and brown people to do without certain of the so-called protective foods that fair-skinned people need wherever they live. That matter awaits proper investigation. But we may safely say that both these factors correspond with an advantage, to the African worker, as compared with the English worker of, at the very most, 20 per cent. If, in other words, African workers are to be as efficient and healthy in body and mind as English workers are, they must have incomes at least 80 per cent. of those that English workers have. Instead, as we have seen, family incomes in one African country that is under the control of Imperial Parliament average about 4 per cent. of the ordinary English standard, and in another, where admittedly the poverty is exceptional, even for East Africa, they average only 2 per cent.

It may be best to raise here another question. Large

importations of capital, as a principal remedy for African poverty, are advocated by men, some of whom have had long and wide African experience. The prescription should not lightly be set aside, even by those who believe that capitalism is the root of all evil. The plight of those Nyasalanders who grow tobacco, whose industry needs little capital equipment, proves that the familiar Marxist analysis fails to explain the facts. It is, of course, true that in industries such as cocoa-growing, that needs European capital only for transport, the worker, in theory, ought to be better off than in industries that need much capital on which profit must be earned. But those cocoa farmers in the Gold Coast employ labourers just as English farmers do, at wages which, though double those that Kenya planters pay, are still deplorably low. And are we to decide that wealth should lie undisturbed in the ground because its extraction is impossible without large capital expenditure? It must also be borne in mind that Socialism is impossible in contemporary Africa, since Socialists do not exist in it. State capitalism, of course, is a practicable solution. But one would suggest that all such questions as the form capital should take, and whether in this case or that a mine should be sunk, with the result that peasants are eventually turned into a proletariat, are secondary. If men were sent to govern in Africa with a conception of their duty quite different from the conception of it that has been held by the men who have made East Africa what it now is, all such questions would answer themselves. It may even be doubted whether this whole group of questions about European capital in Africa ought primarily to be regarded from the African point of view. The migration of capital from Europe and

America to less civilized parts of the world has worldwide implications and results. The man who used to mine copper in the United States for five dollars a day, but who now finds himself unemployed because his master transferred some of his capital to Rhodesia, where he pays miners 1s. a day, has at least as much right as anyone else to decide questions of mineral exploitation in Africa. This is no place to discuss that wider problem. But we ought all to think it out for ourselves.

CHAPTER VII

EUROPEAN TAXATION AND RELATED MATTERS

TANGANYIKA, Kenya and Uganda form a Customs Union. But they as well as the other countries in British East Africa have different laws about the direct taxation of non-Africans. In Kenya, an income tax came into force only in 1937, after an intermittent struggle that lasted nearly twenty years between the Colonial Office and the settlers supported by the local Government. But the law actually enacted in Nairobi so completely defeated the intention of the Colonial Office that, in the first year in which the tax was in full operation, only one European landowner in seven paid any income tax at all. This inadequate taxation of the rich and the relatively rich is a feature common to nearly all the countries of the Colonial Empire. It was intended to show the facts of the matter in tables, in which it could be seen at a glance what people with the same incomes have to pay in various colonies as compared with the rates in the United Kingdom. But the construction of accurate tables was found to be impossible. Rates of taxation change not only frequently but at different dates in different colonies. And differences in matters so important as a wife's allowance cannot be stated in tabular form. So illustrative examples are all that can be given here. They are all taken from a valuable summary in the Colonial Office library that ought to be published and widely known.

EUROPEAN TAXATION AND RELATED MATTERS

In considering the figures that follow it should be borne in mind that the " cost of living " is higher in Africa than in Europe. The reason for the inverted commas is that the words, like the phrase " standard of living," conceal a falsehood. When we consider the sums on which Africans subsist it seems sheer irony to say that it costs a European more to live in Africa than at home. Yet in a real sense it does. The most unjustly high indirect taxation, to which we shall come shortly, has results that perhaps ought not to be included in the cost of living. What must also be reckoned with is the fact that every European who enters Africa finds himself presented with a patent of nobility. He belongs to an aristocracy of birth, and on all hands is expected to have servants from whom he keeps his distance. Those very servants, a numerous class in the richer colonies, look down on a man who does not keep a proper establishment, and has not all the right kinds of refreshment on his board. Their nickname for one well-known man was " one plate." There are some Europeans, it is true, who do not live up to their position. In East Africa a poor white class is growing up that is blind to the fact that, as in South Africa, its own poverty is the result of Africans' poverty, to which colour bars contribute so largely. Apart, however, from so incalculable an ingredient as prestige in the cost of living, the cost of transport from the sea adds greatly to the prices of all imported goods in many African countries. On the other hand local produce, such as eggs and vegetables, is cheap up-country and the wages of domestics are low. On balance a fair estimate would make the cost of living from all causes in Northern Rhodesia a quarter more than in Britain, and rather less in the highlands of Kenya. So that an income of £550 in the

Kenya highlands and one of £600 in Northern Rhodesia would go about as far as one of £500 in Britain.

Readers who dislike the trouble of studying figures may prefer to be told what the figures that follow mean rather than read them themselves. Thirty-two British Colonies, or about half the total, have no income tax at all. In some others the rate can only be called derisory. In Ceylon, for instance, an income of £4,750 pays only a shilling in the pound. In most of the older colonies that have an income tax liability begins at much the same level as with us and the allowances for wife and children are much the same. The great difference lies in the rate per pound of the tax. In those older colonies the net amount payable is from a fifth to a twentieth of what it is here. But in the colour bar countries of East Africa, not only is the rate per pound quite as much less as in the older colonies. Liability to the tax begins at a much higher level, so that five out of every six people who here are taxed escape altogether. And allowances are twice or thrice as generous as with us.

All the figures in brackets in the typical instances that follow show the tax payable on the same incomes in Britain. To take first one of the older colonies, in Barbados liability begins at £150 or £250 for a married man. On the next £200 the rate per pound is 3d. and it rises by 3d. for every £200 up to an income of £1,250. So that a married man with no children pays £3 15s. (£92 16s. 3d.) on an income of £500, and on one of £1,000, £22 10s. (£280 6s. 3d.). Barbados has not so far increased the pre-war rate. Jamaica has. There, liability used to start at £300, the rate on the next £100 was 2½d., and gradual increases similar to those in Barbados brought the tax on an income of £500 to £2 5s. 10d. and on one of £1,000 to

£17 18s. 4d. Increased rates since the war started have raised those sums to £7 5s. 10d. (£92 16s. 3d.) and £30 8s. 4d. (£280 6s. 3d.) respectively. These are figures typical of the incidence of income tax in colonies acquired before the 1880's. By contrast, in Northern Rhodesia a wife's allowance, until recently £600, is now £380 and a man with a wife and one child pays no tax unless he has more than £700 a year. A man similarly circumstanced with £1,000 a year pays £11 5s. (£261 11s. 3d.). In Kenya nominal rates were last year rather higher and recently they were further increased by 40 per cent. But the proportion of people in that country, apart from salaried officials, who escape paying income tax altogether is so high that the printed figures are not worth quoting. In Tanganyika the clause in the constitution that prohibits racial discrimination has not prevented the Government from taxing Africans and non-Africans by separate laws. A childless married European in that country with £500 pays no income tax at all (£92 16s. 3d.). If he has an income of £1,000 he pays £9 16s. (£280 6s. 3d.).

It is quite true that the wealthy minorities in the colonies are small. But the sums spent in them on educational, sanitary and other social services are so trifling that, in the case of many countries, an income tax with an incidence only half as heavy as in Britain would enable their Governments to treble their expenditure on social services. Why then is that not done? There is only one possible answer in the most glaring cases, the countries of East Africa, which is that rich residents in them refuse to be taxed for the benefit of the poor, because those poor are Africans. But that is not an adequate reason, since policy, in those East African countries, is determined by Governors chosen by the Colonial Office, which is responsible in turn to Parliament and the nation. Here then is plain proof that Governors take their policy from the resident European minorities. And the reason they are allowed to do so is that public opinion in Britain is apathetic. It is apathetic because it is not informed.

In most East African countries there is a European poll tax, with a complicated history; that in Kenya is at present £2 10s. Years ago, those who were so destitute as to be unable to pay the poll tax were shipped to Bombay and deposited there. The writer has been unable to find out what happens to such men now. We may at least be sure that not for them is the month's labour in a " detention camp." Death duties that bring in £4,000 to £6,000 a year complete the tale of the direct taxation to which in Kenya Europeans are liable.

Not only the settlers, but the local authorities claim that the very heavy indirect taxation that Europeans, and Indians, have to pay makes up for the lack of any substantial direct taxation. Only in Africa could such a claim be made. It is universally recognized everywhere else that high import duties on what to Europeans and Asiatics are the necessities of life hardly touch the rich, but bear heavily on the poor, especially on those with dependants. The poorer people are, moreover, and the more dependants they have, the larger is the proportion of their incomes that a tariff of that type compels them to pay in taxation. The poorest people of all, the Africans, pay hardly any indirect taxation, since by the time they have paid their direct taxation, they have little left over to buy anything with. The author tried to work out, from the trade returns, the value per head of the combined African population of Kenya and Uganda of the imported goods they consume. At most, it comes to 2s. When customs duties, cost of transport to the interior, and retailers' profits are added, that sum of 2s., the price at Mombasa-Kilindini, the port of entry, will have become about 5s. These figures may be out by as much even as 50 per cent. On the other hand, it may be no accident that if we multiply the 5s. by five to turn expenditure per head into expenditure per family, we get a sum not much less than the 30s., which according to the author's estimate, or 36s. according to the official figures, the average African family in Kenya has left over after paying the hut and poll tax. It is worth noting that trade goods for African consumption, such as calico, cotton blankets and hoes, are charged railway freights four, six or even ten times the rates that are charged on plantation products for export.

The Kenya-Uganda tariff heavily taxes not only luxuries but all the articles necessary to civilized life, clothing, furniture and hardware, as well as flour and every sort of foodstuff. But its most remarkable feature is its free list. That list includes goods valued at 40 per cent. of the total imports. In any ordinary country it would consist of the goods that the poorest must, or ought to be encouraged to, consume, tinned milk and calico for instance. But none of such things is exempt from duty. Books and drugs are the only items on the free list that conceivably might, to some extent, reach Africans' hands. Instead, the free list is almost entirely composed of articles that only Europeans buy, especially those of them who have land, such as lorries, machinery and fencing materials. That illustrates how one comes across colour bars round every corner in East Africa, bars of which, fortunately for us, hardly any Africans are aware. All East African life in epitome lies in the facts that the bicycle to be used by the peasant in Uganda who grows cotton is taxed, while the European landowner's tractor is admitted duty free, and that the cotton the peasant grows is carried to the sea on the State railway at a rate per ton three times as great as is charged on the tractor-grown wheat and maize. Hardly any East Africans can afford artificial light. The few use candles. The candles they use pay a higher duty than those intended for use in mining gold. A handful of European stock farmers exports a few tons of butter. They are subsidized by an addition to the price of all the butter consumed inside the country. The 30 per cent. tariff on wheat and flour has the same purpose and result.

It is quite possible that the poorer half of the Europeans in Kenya, and nearly all the Indians, are now making a contribution to revenue as large as is just. The remarkable thing is that those people do not see that some part of the high price of what they buy goes, not into the coffers of the State, but into the pockets of their richer countrymen, who pay a vastly less proportion of their incomes to the State than they do. So much stronger and hotter-blooded than the motive of gain is that other motive, that we call racial arrogance and lust of domination when displayed in Europe, but describe more indulgently when our countrymen act upon it in Africa.

This book is about colour bars, not about their converse, the privileges and subsidies that Europeans in East Africa enjoy. The instances of unfair advantages that have come to our notice suggest a doubt whether, if they were done away with, " white settlement " would survive. Would it not therefore be wise for the Colonial Office to discourage, if not to prohibit, further European immigration into East Africa ? As these words are being written the news comes that British taxpayers are to give

British Colonies £5,000,000 a year. The largest item on the first list of the objects on which the money is to be spent is the cost, just over £5,000,000, of the Kenya and Uganda railway. We are, it seems, to make a present of that railway to the taxpayers of East Africa, or rather to our countrymen there who have so far managed to escape the taxation we inflict on ourselves. One would suggest that grants from this new fund should be made conditional on the taxation of the recipients at the same rate as the givers of the money.

Some readers may wish to know what is the constitutional position of the European minorities in these East African countries. It varies with the proportion of Europeans in the population. At one end of the constitutional scale is Southern Rhodesia. The constitution that in 1923 was given to that country, when Mr. Churchill was at the Colonial Office, contained no trace of a colour bar. The right of Africans to own land anywhere was specifically asserted in it. But one of Mr. Churchill's successors allowed a change in the constitution that has enabled the Government to make it illegal for Africans to own or lease land in the more eligible and practically all the well-watered parts of the country, the parts that contain all the mines and are well supplied with roads and railways, and include all the towns. Ownership of land, in those parts, is restricted to the 66,000 Europeans. Such of the African population of just over a million as live in them may lawfully do so only if they are in European employment. This arrangement is called segregation. That term is grossly misleading. The great majority of the inhabitants of the parts of the country where only Europeans may own land are Africans. As in Kenya, it is not their presence that pollutes the air, but their existence in them as freemen. The parts left in African occupation are, as Mr. Roy Macgregor's forthcoming book will show, rocky, arid and almost devoid of roads. Though huge in area, so small and crowded are the places where cultivation is possible, that already the Government has had to float a loan for their irrigation and for the reclamation of their eroded soil.

Among the laws of Southern Rhodesia there is one that subsidizes the price of exported maize by raising the price of maize consumed in the country. This Act set up a Maize Board with the sole right of buying maize, and lays down a sliding scale according to which the price the Board pays a man for his maize depends on the amount he has to sell. Thus a man with 10,000 bags to sell gets much less per bag than a man with only 1,000, and he again less than the man with only 100. (Small farmers in Rhodesia, being the majority, have more votes than big farmers.) No African ever has as much maize to sell as the smallest European farmers have. Yet the Act ordains that the Board is to pay Africans with maize to sell the same price as it pays Europeans with the largest amount to sell, that is, the lowest price.

Africans mined gold for centuries in what now is Rhodesia. They do it still, but only as workers for Europeans. None is even allowed a prospector's licence. Not a penny has ever been paid for the wholesale expropriation of land and mines in Rhodesia. In that country colour bars are as numerous and as impossible to surmount as they are in the Union of South Africa, where many modern colour bars originated. Finally, by requiring a high property qualification for the franchise, and perhaps by subtler means as well, Africans in Southern Rhodesia are kept off voters' rolls so effectively that by the last account only about sixty of them have votes.

The constitution of Southern Rhodesia requires its Government to submit legislation that affects African interests to the Colonial Office. How futile that proviso has been under recent Secretaries of State is evident from the fact that Northern Rhodesia, that is completely under the control of Downing Street and Parliament, was allowed to copy the Act that in Southern Rhodesia regulates the prices that various parties are paid for maize. The Governors of all the countries of British East Africa except Southern Rhodesia have absolute power, when they wish to use it. They may, that is to say, and sometimes do, order the official majorities in their Legislatures to vote as they direct. That is not to say that they often use their power. Most of them play for safety by pleasing the men who have been to the right schools, wear the right clothes and play the right games. But why does that course bring safety?

In Nyasaland, Tanganyika and Uganda, the Governor nominates those whom he thinks best to a minority of the seats in his Legislature. In Kenya Europeans elect, by adult suffrage, a large minority of the Legislature. Twice as many Indians elect fewer than half as many representatives. No African has a vote, though many Africans in Kenya, not, of course, the illiterate majority, would use votes as intelligently as most Europeans do. It may be the existence in Kenya of so many titled and beribboned people that has given Kenya settlers undeserved notoriety. An unusual proportion of them does belong to that class of people who assume that when they touch a bell whatever they may want is brought them by the operations of Nature. But the fact deserves to be stated that many of them make determined efforts to be just. More than once, indeed, they have opposed their Government in defence of Africans' interests, and have exposed abuses of authority. They cannot be expected to recognize that they are in an impossible situation. To blame them for being in that position is unjust. Rather does the blame rest on recent Colonial Governors and Secretaries of State, on Parliament and on the British electorate. Culpable ignorance of history probably does more than anything else to explain why in East Africa we have drifted so far from the older British policy. For the experiment of settling Northern Europeans in the tropics was made three centuries ago. Two centuries ago the population of Jamaica was still mainly British, and the records of the time, not perhaps very reliable, show that the Colony could raise a militia of 15,000 men for the French wars. No part of that Island is more than 40 miles from the sea, whereas in the case of the Kenya highlands the distance is from 300 to 500 miles. To-day in Jamaica, out of a population of 1,150,000, persons of pure European descent, though still owning the bulk of the land, form only 1.5 per cent. of the inhabitants.

CHAPTER VIII

MINES

NEITHER in East nor in South Africa is the soil ever likely to produce great wealth and support a large population as it does in Europe. Indeed a recent Commission estimated that in South Africa the fertility of the soil had fallen by a half in the previous hundred years. On the other hand the continent does contain vast deposits of diamonds, gold, copper and other minerals. In East Africa the most important of them are the deposits of copper that extend across Northern Rhodesia into the Belgian Congo.

To Africans of this generation those mines are of little account. The reason is not that so little of the wealth they produce goes to them, although, as we shall see in a moment, that is true enough. It is rather that life seems and feels unnatural when spent apart from the land. Yet the great size of those copper deposits, the haste with which they are being exploited, and the methods used in the exploitation, seem to make certain the rise of an African proletariat. Only in South Africa has that happened so far. Elsewhere, except for a few thousand families in the Belgian Congo, where the Government, much to its credit, is trying the experiment of giving miners permanent homes in villages near the mines, employment in mines is temporary. Men work in them for two, four, twelve or more months and then go home to their villages.

The mining of copper in Rhodesia began only after the great war. The main economic facts about the mines are as follows. They all relate to the year 1937 :—

Dividends of from 20 per cent. to 80 per cent. were paid of more than £5,000,000
Royalties to the British South Africa Co. of over £500,000
Taxation of about £700,000
The salaries of 1,690 Europeans amounted to about £800,000
The wages paid to African miners, of whom 17,000 were in employment on any given date, were £244,000

While the average salaried European is thus seen to have an income of about £500, and the average African miner an income of about £17 (if continuously employed), no African gets a wage that is more than a fraction of the salary of the lowest-paid European.

In that same year, 1937, some 28,000, or about one in six of the African children in Northern Rhodesia, went to the schools of Christian Missions. No others are open to them. In grants to those schools the Government spent £33,000, or about 4s. per child of school age and 24s. per child at school. On the education of the 1,045 European children in the country it spent £38,000, or £37 per child. The disparity is defended on the ground of prestige, because at all cost the rise of a class of " poor whites " must be prevented. That means that a secure position in the ruling caste must be found for the stupidest man of European descent, but no place above the servile for the most gifted African.

A later chapter will describe in fuller detail this educational colour bar, as it stands to-day in Kenya. Here we may observe that this particular colour bar, of all colour bars the most fertile in injustice and the most dangerous to social order, exists, in the Empire, only in the countries of South and East Africa. But social diseases are as infectious as microbic. Officials trained in East Africa are promoted to posts of authority in other parts of the Empire. Only last year much offence was caused in the West Indies by an advertisement of a post specifying that applicants must be of pure British descent.

It is this educational colour bar which, together with their ignorance, until so recently, of any way of life except the tribal, explains the silence of East Africans. The mental anæmia thus doubly caused, combined too often with a subnormal level of physical health, makes thinking impossible to many.

No reader is likely to approve of the way the wealth produced in those copper mines is allocated. But the fault does not lie with the mining companies. It is their recognised duty to pay the most they can in dividends and the least they can in taxes. The wages they pay are more than double the rate paid by other employers in the country. The tribes from which the miners come were the last to be overtaken by, and delivered from, the Arab slavers. Hardly had they come back from their hiding places, when another world force uprooted them. It is our need of copper for reading by electric light on winter evenings that draws them out of the dull quiet of village life and plunges them into the strife of modern competitive industry. Under those two successive blows, social disintegration, as all observers testify, has gone farther than it has in the case of any other East African tribes. The Missions have dropped their differences to make a common effort to check the disintegration, but so far the Government seems to have made no such effort. Rare indeed, it must be admitted, are the qualities that fit men and women for so thankless a task. The petty crime, prostitution, gambling and contempt for authority, their own tribal authority as well as ours, are probably due, in some measure, to the kind of quarters that the companies provide for the miners. Eye-witnesses say that most of the mining villages were laid out without regard for the needs of African life. African huts, with mud-walls, thatched roofs, and space under the eaves for air to circulate, are cool at midday and warm at night. The mining companies put up, as most employers in East Africa do, shells of brick or concrete, with galvanised iron roofs, that are stifling in the midday sun and cold at night. They built those square shells in immensely long rows, each exactly like the rest, which is what Africans particularly abominate. Worse still, they allowed no room for gardens, and gardens are as truly necessities to Africans as tables and chairs are to us. Worst of all, they cut down all the trees. And that in African eyes was not only the destruction of shade but desecration. An engineer fresh from England could not be expected to understand the discomfort he was creating, and the sacrilege he was committing, especially when his fellows regarded Africans as sub-human. But surely the Governor must have had at his disposal men well able to advise the companies on such matters.

Opinions will naturally differ as to how much of the six millions that now go to shareholders and royalty-owners ought to be spent on benefits to the people of the country. The Johannesburg Chamber of Mines estimates that the Government of the Union of South Africa takes

46 per cent. of the profits of mining gold in that country. If the Government of Northern Rhodesia took the same proportion of the profits of those copper mines, it could provide schools for all the children in the country. Schools, because, as our own national history shows, popular education is what arrests the social disintegration that attends an industrial revolution, builds up the social fabric, and is the only safe basis for material prosperity. Why, then, is that not done?

Gold mining in Kenya has not so far brought large profits to the companies engaged in it. So moderate a tax as 5 per cent. on the value of gold exported was therefore, perhaps, not unreasonable. It just covered the cost of running the Kenya Mines Department. In January, 1938, the Government announced that, for no given reason, the tax would be levied no longer. The fact is mentioned merely to show who the people are whom the Government chooses to be the recipients of its bounty. Since the war broke out the tax has been reimposed.

The last chapter of this book has been given the form of a dispatch from some future Secretary of State to the Governors of British Dependencies in Africa, instructing them how to apply, how rather to restore, the old policy of equal rights. That form was chosen because it enables us to get as close as possible to the real difficulties. The dispatch, accordingly, contains an exposition of the most vital and critical measures involved by the change of policy. But it may be as well, at this stage, to explore the consequences to some of the colour bars we have examined of the change of policy.

First in regard to taxation. No immediate change would of necessity be brought about in indirect taxation.

If in course of time political change brought about a change in the minds of administrators, so that they came to consider an African labourer as important a person as a European landowner, extensive changes would take place in such things, for example, as the articles that are admitted free of duty. But that is an instance of the ultimate results of the change. An immediate result would be seen in direct taxation. Under a single fiscal system the hut and poll tax would at once be seen to be what it is, an income tax, an income tax, moreover, with an incidence in proportion to income vastly higher than the incidence of the tax paid by even the richest European. What is equally indefensible is that the incidence varies as between individual taxpayers, not in proportion to their wealth, but in proportion to their unavoidable expenditure, so that the more mouths a man has to feed, the more taxes he has to pay. The application of the policy of equal rights would make both these glaring injustices manifest, as now they are not. Morally, of course, there is no case at all for any direct taxation whatever of people so poor as we have found East Africans to be. But if, as one is always told, some compromise must be sought for, to make gradual the application of the policy of equal rights, much the best substitute for the hut and poll tax would be a tax on wages. It would be a tax on salaries in its higher ranges and would be graduated. It would be so much easier to collect than the hut and poll tax that it would reduce the cost of administration by many thousands of pounds.

The hut and poll tax now in force in the six countries in British East Africa brings in from 12 per cent. to 30 per cent. of their total revenue from taxation. The author calculates that if the rate of income tax and surtax in force in the United Kingdom in May 1940 were in force in Kenya, with an all-round reduction of 25 per cent. to cover the higher cost of living, the additional revenue would amount to over 60 per cent. of the £700,000 that Africans now pay in direct taxation.

In regard to land, at first sight it would seem that it was too late to apply the policy of equal rights, for, as we saw, the land is gone. Yet there is much that might be done without injury to those Europeans who not only deserve the reward of hard work but also do service by their example to their African neighbours. The Crown could resume the ownership of derelict estates at small cost. A tax on undeveloped land, for which there are many precedents, would bring much of it into the market. The land thus acquired should be used for family holdings of from ten to fifty acres. We may grant that large communal holdings may in time prove a better system, both as a method of producing wealth and socially. And if there is money to spare, experiments in that direction might be made immediately. But what ought at once to be done is to satisfy the demand that most Africans in every country make, for land of their own, land that if not legally is at any rate securely theirs. Such family holdings would, of course, be suitably grouped, to give each access to a road, to water and to a school. And one would hazard the suggestion that each group should contain members of different tribes. In face of inevitable tribal disintegration, everything possible should be done to encourage social reintegration.

The policy of equal rights would result in some immediate economy in budgets, by enabling Africans to do, at much less cost, much work that Europeans, and in some cases Indians, do now. Ultimately, equality of educational opportunity would lead to the admission of Africans to salaried posts, and transform East African society.

Readers should work out for themselves what the effect would be on various other colour bars of giving people equal rights. They will be astonished to find how many positive results ensue directly from the principle. Indeed, of the specific reforms that the situation cries out for, many would be brought about by, and all would be rendered easier by, the patient but determined application of the policy of prohibiting distinctions on the ground of race or colour, in both a country's laws and in its administration.

Appendix to Chapter VIII

In March 1940 seventeen African miners were killed and seventy wounded by rifle fire during disturbances at two of the three copper mines in Northern Rhodesia. The Governor appointed a Commission of Inquiry into the matter. When its report reached the Colonial Office Mr. Creech Jones, M.P., asked for its publication. The request was refused on the ground that the Governor's comments on the report had not been received. At the time of writing, October 1940, the report is still unpublished. But the following account may be relied upon as accurate.

On March 18th the European employees at Nkana and Mufulira went on strike. (They have a trade union but it was not concerned in the strike.) The Government intervened, conciliation followed and on March 27th the strike was settled, the men winning most of what they had asked for. On March 29th all except a few hundred of the 15,000 Africans employed at the same two mines went on strike. The Government did not intervene, nor was there any attempt at conciliation. Troops and armed police were called out, and when on the sixth day of the strike the strikers interfered with some 150 strike breakers who were getting their wages, they fired tear gas bombs on the crowd. The infuriated men made a rush at the building where the Europeans had gathered and the troops opened fire to defend them. Next day the men were back at work.

The Commission of Inquiry contained a representative of the European employees of the mining companies but no African. The evidence of the mining companies and managers was submitted in writing and was not made public. The mine and compound managers made only a formal appearance before the Commission, preferring to leave their case in the hands of a K.C. from Johannesburg. The African witnesses gave their evidence orally and in public, and, though cross-examined, had no legal adviser.

No industrial organization exists among those African copper miners. Instead, the Government has set up a kind of offshoot of the tribal organization, the members of each tribe appointing their own " elders." During the strike the chief of the largest tribe sent a message, no doubt under direction, from several hundred miles away, ordering the men to go back to work. That illustrates how " indirect rule " comes to be the attempt to confine Africans to their own past, an attempt that springs from the belief, or rather the assumption, that they are sub-human. The demand for higher wages was in the forefront of the strikers' demands, but complaints were also made about housing and food. One gathers that the real issue of the strike, the colour bar, though fully recognized as such by all concerned, was plainly stated by one only of the men who gave evidence before the Commission.

Perhaps the most significant episode in these events was the challenge the strikers made when the strike began. They asked to be allowed to work a shift by themselves in competition with Europeans, to prove who do the real work of mining and how useless most of the European supervisors are.

The evidence given at the inquiry showed that already a large proportion of these copper miners have so completely abandoned their homes in distant villages that they never even visit them. This large and increasing proportion of the miners is the vanguard of a new African proletariat, that has neither tribal rights nor tribal obligations, and with no homes other than those provided by their employers.

CHAPTER IX

POLITICS

AS this book is written, and should be read, with the eye on the end of the telescope opposite to the end commonly used, that word politics is here taken to mean the experience in government of the governed. On the first arrival of a responsible British agent at any place in Africa, the attendance of the chief was demanded. Expecting the worst, people often put forward whoever could best be spared. Thus nobodies or men even less regarded found themselves turned into chiefs overnight. Tribes that had none were provided with chiefs. The astonishing thing is that choices so farcical were so often successful. One very able Kikuyu paramount chief began life as the Commissioner's donkey-boy. In most cases of course real effort was made to discover and respect traditional authority. The trouble was that it was so indeterminate. The only true answer to the question what, in the case of any given tribe, were the duties of chief, council, the women, the general body of the tribe, was, "it all depends." The one thing that an administrator must have was a tribal head, some one man to whom he could give orders, with the result that the tribe would obey them. In consequence the whole influence of British agents was exerted to aggrandise the power of the chief, and to leave out of account both that of the populace, which, even if rarely used, played on important issues the preponderant part, and that of the women, even when symbolized, as in some West African tribes, by a queen-mother who often was the power behind the throne. Thus from the first the insistent and insoluble question arose, whether the chief was to continue to be the tribal mouthpiece, or whether he was to be the executive agent of an alien Government, whose main duty was to transmit and enforce its orders. The incident about to be recounted will best make clear the transformation that both the powers and duties of chiefs, and the tribes' conception of their position, have undergone. Naturally that transformation was most rapid and complete where, as in Kenya, the orders that the chiefs had to transmit were least welcome, orders, namely, for labour at once, and for the tax money soon afterwards. Thus in East and parts of West Africa, " Native Authorities " in fact became, what in law they all are, the lowest grade in the official hierarchy. In Kenya, though not in Tanganyika, the D.O. is even the chairman and secretary of the N.A. and has an over-riding power that makes his decision the decision of the N.A., whatever the wishes of the other members. That is an extreme case of one type, and we may hope that power so arbitrary is never used. The extreme case of the opposite type is seen in the Gold Coast, where the " States " claim an independence that is modified by the terms of treaties made a century ago. There, under the influence of the school that teaches that learning from Europe is an evil thing to be shunned, N.A.s have undergone a process of fossilizing. Until recently, for now less obscurantist ideas prevail, the ideal aimed at was pure conservatism. At council meetings rival families struggled for offices that no longer carried any useful function with them, argued over rank and precedent, and performed ceremonies in words of which the meaning sometimes was lost. The stool-bearer who stands behind every important chief on great occasions must carry his stool aslant, in case some demon finds lodgement on it and disturbs the general harmony. The paradoxical result is that it is just where " functional " anthropologists have had their way, and Africans have been persuaded sacredly to cherish their own institutions, that they value them least, and turn instead to Government Departments for what they need in the modern world, schools, health services, better agriculture and the rest. The Gold Coast is in a ferment now, out of which, it is safe to predict, whatever may emerge, the obsolete will not. It used to supply the world with most of its cocoa. Now, thanks to Herr Hitler, much of the crop is unsaleable and, since it will not keep long, has had to be burnt.

No chimaera bombinans in vacuo is more elusive than indirect rule. Volumes of controversy on the subject already exist. But for several reasons we may regard the Native Authorities that Sir Donald Cameron set up in Tanganyika as the orthodox variety. It is generally agreed that his N.A.s worked better than any other Governor's. He has told us in a book what his ideal N.A. is, what powers and duties the actual N.A.s had under his Governorship of Tanganyika, and even, with unusual candour, how in some cases his N.A.s had been allowed to run off the rails after he left the country. And the Colonial Office seems to be inviting other Governors of African countries to copy the type of N.A. that Sir Donald designed.

Sir Donald insists, rightly, that the term indirect rule is a complete misnomer. It is indeed another of those calamitous phrases, of which we have noted other instances already, that mislead the public mind. In Sir

Donald's view an N.A. is simply an organ of local government, that differs from such organs elsewhere as the result of the fact that African society is tribal. But Sir Donald was determined that his N.A.s should have real work to do, and that no tenderness to the merely traditional should stand in the way of their efficiency. He saw that the tribal institutions that had survived from the past must be adapted both to enable them to do the work he wanted them to do and to attract the popular support without which that work could not be done. Some semblance with the past must be preserved. As little as possible must be recognizably new, and as little offence given to ancient loyalties and deferences. Nor did Sir Donald lay down any minimum conditions to be complied with, far less any standard pattern for his N.A.s. Hence their constitution varied greatly. All had some sort of Council. But while many Councils were subordinate to some chief who had already become a petty monarch, others were given real executive authority, and some were in part even elected. The Council of one important group of tribes was given no head at all, except its annually elected chairman. Sir Donald endowed his N.A.s by returning to them from a third to a tenth of what the tribe had paid in hut tax, the proportion depending on the range of duties that each N.A. was entrusted with. And he gave them real though limited independence by forbidding D.O.s to interfere with their decisions, reserving that right to himself alone. But the accounts of N.A.s' Treasuries were audited by a Government auditor. One wonders whether in giving most N.A.s a mainly autocratic rather than a mainly popular and elective character Sir Donald wanted to avoid the aspersion of Europeanizing. The duties that Sir Donald gave N.A.s included the erection and management of schools, sanitation and waterworks, maternity and child-welfare work, bush clearance to keep down tsetse fly, the upkeep of roads and bridges, and the collection of the hut tax.

Such was the kind of N.A. Sir Donald Cameron set up in Tanganyika. Elsewhere in British Africa different types exist, the differences arising from the level of civilization at which a tribe has attained, and on the ideas of administrators. The story about to be told will give a far better idea than any analysis of the difficulties that beset " indirect rule " of whatever pattern. But before it is told we should recognize that the imbalance those difficulties reveal, that is acknowledged by the most ardent advocates of indirect rule, is of necessity inherent. For every N.A. is poised between forces that cannot be expected to harmonize. There is, first, the tribal opinion which, as elsewhere in the world, is increasingly divided between the old school and the new. There is beneficent authority as exemplified by Sir Donald himself, who prescribed exactly what N.A.s were to do, with more right than most, since he did on occasion take a stand in defence of Africans' interests. And finally, there is the more usual type of Governor, whose policy in all its ramifications, that extend even to his relations with N.A.s, is based on satisfying the wishes of resident Europeans.

Even before the Great War German missionaries had introduced the coffee tree to the Chagga tribe, that lives on the lower slopes of Kilimanjaro in Tanganyika. But it was only on the disappearance of the German planters during the war that their Chagga labourers started to grow coffee on a large scale for themselves. In a few years some 24,000 of them were growing it, selling it to Indian traders, and getting for it far more than they could earn in wages, either in Tanganyika, or in near-by Kenya. This development displeased the mainly British planters who had replaced the Germans. Across the border, in Kenya, coffee-growing was, and for ten years later continued to be, a strict European monopoly—in practice it still is. Indeed, if ever a colour bar can be defended, it is in this case. Coffee is no fool's crop like wheat. The berry has to be skilfully pulped, dried and fermented on the farm, before the kernels are sent to the curing factory. Also graded coffee may fetch 50 per cent. more than a mixed consignment that still has the same average quality, so that one parcel of dirty or otherwise inferior coffee, the contribution of a single careless African, might cost the other contributors hundreds of pounds. Finally, the coffee tree is subject to several diseases that already are endemic in Africa, and so can be kept in check only by the spraying and banding of every tree. The reason the Kenya planters gave for inducing their Government to refuse licences to grow coffee to Africans was that they were too uncivilized to be trusted to obey the regulations of the Agricultural Department. Unfortunately for those planters, the action of the Kenya Government in allowing them that monopoly was publicly challenged in the author's first book, published in 1924, and by that time large numbers of Africans were producing coffee from trees even of the delicate variety in both Tanganyika and Uganda. Stimulated by the example and urgings of their fellows in Kenya the planters in Tanganyika, though not in Uganda, demanded the same monopoly. Sir Donald Cameron had just been appointed Governor. He stoutly rejected the demand, and made himself for a time the best-hated man in East Africa by giving active help to the Chagga in the organizing of their industry. The Provincial Commissioner,

Dundas, had the confidence of the tribe. He and several equally enthusiastic men in the Agricultural Department founded the Kilimanjaro Native Planters' Association. The settlers protested to the Colonial Office, but in vain. For several years the K.N.P.A. was a huge success. (Prices happened to stay high.) The Director of Agriculture reported that the quality of the Association's coffee was quite as good as the planters'.

But the Association contained within it the seed of its dissolution. Being a genuinely popular body, it had to conform with its members' wishes. Now Africans hate rules and regulations, especially since they are not understood, nor are even, in most East African countries, translated into the vernaculars. And East African Governments, as in all countries where the wishes of the common people are not enquired into, take pleasure in making regulations. So to those Chagga all rules were at best nuisances, snags on which you stub your toe when you least expect it. They therefore objected to membership cards, and still more to anything so suspiciously like a tax as share capital. The most they could be persuaded to were an annual subscription of 1s. and a 2 per cent. levy on sales to cover marketing costs. The only penalty for the breach of such rules as there were was expulsion. On the other hand they insisted on paying the members of the elected committee relatively enormous salaries—in one case £120—so as to be more than upsides with the Chagga N.A., that happened to be more traditional and less popular and representative than most. Though thus unprepared for trouble, the K.N.P.A. might gradually have built up a reserve fund and adopted more orthodox business methods if official help had been continued. But when Cameron left the country for Nigeria, the settlers renewed their demand to the Colonial Office that it should be withdrawn, this time with success. Dundas was transferred elsewhere. To the members of the committee, now on their own, all such matters as transport and marketing were unimagined mysteries—remember that no boy in Tanganyika is taught what all our children learn before they leave school. Gradually a rot set in. One committee member was said to have levanted with £1,000. (His case is obscure. He seems never to have been brought to trial.) Indian traders tempted people to sell their coffee to them rather than to the K.N.P.A. Coffee stealing became a trade like boot-legging in America. By 1929 the Association was handling only half the coffee crop, and in 1930 it was bankrupt. The D.O. was instructed to take temporary charge of what was left of it.

In this quandary the Government turned to compulsion as the only way out. Its difficulty was that the constitution of the country, which is governed under mandate, prohibits legislation that discriminates on the ground of race. And the European coffee-planters were adamant in refusing to enter any body containing African members with rights the same as their own. So in deference to their opposition the Government withdrew the bill it had introduced to set up a monopoly organization.

Then the Government passed into law a copy of a South African Act, that regulates co-operative societies, and gives them, under certain conditions, the sole right to buy the staple crop of a district. It then turned the K.N.P.A. into the Kilimanjaro Native Co-operative Union, and provided the Union with the set of model rules laid down by the new law, rules which the Chagga would have strongly objected to if they had been consulted.

Even then, the Government found that a three to one majority of the Union's members was needed, under the terms of the new law, before the Union could be given a legal monopoly. And that was not to be hoped for. Nor could the Government be sure that the Courts, in view of the new law's restricted application to Africans, would find it was *intra vires* and enable Chagga who refused to sell their coffee to the Union to be punished.

So as a last resort the Government decided to make use of its power over the Native Authority, and told the Chagga N.A. to pass a rule, that came to be known as the Chagga rule, compelling all the members of the tribe to sell their coffee to the K.N.C.U. The Chagga N.A. was nothing loath. It had watched, in the growth of the K.N.P.A., a rival that had left it in eclipse. In its heyday that rival had brought unexampled prosperity to nearly 30,000 Chagga families. And it had provided the natural leaders of the tribe with posts that were better paid than the Chagga chiefs themselves were. Inevitably, therefore, the measures the Government took from 1929 to 1931 were highly unpopular. As we shall see in a moment, the Government was also very unlucky. The author of the Sessional Paper on the subject that the Government laid before the Legislature a few years later wrote, most significantly, that " he did not try to find out members' wishes, because if they were found to be most adverse to Government, an unwelcome situation would have to be faced by Government." The growing resentment of the Chagga against the Government and their own N.A. was fed from many sources. The K.N.C.U., which was a federation of over twenty local societies, was only in name co-operative. Its real control lay in the hands of the European manager whom the Government had appointed, who was paid £700 a year, and spent, in a few years, £6,000 on buildings, and nearly £3,000 a year on staff. Coincidently, there came first the great depression, when, though the Chagga coffee crop remained at 1,600 to 1,800 tons, its value fell, between 1932 and 1935, from £60,000 to £35,000, and the average sum growers received fell from 56s. 6d. to 27s. 6d.—before 1929 it had been about 80s. Later, when Brazil abandoned burning coffee to keep the price up, the price of Chagga coffee fell still lower.

Africans are not the only people who fail to distinguish between *post hoc* and *propter hoc*. Those Chagga would not have been human if they had not related their loss of income to the changes that had replaced a committee of their own choosing, paternally guided by Dundas and others, by a European manager, a Registrar, and a new society with a host of new rules about which they had not been consulted but which at the dictation, as everyone knew, of their Government, their N.A. compelled them to obey. Matters were made worse by secrecy. One balance sheet was held up for months, and revealed, when it was published, a loss for the year of £6,000. Popular discontent was expressed at public meetings, that were addressed by members of the former committee and passed resolutions in favour of a return to the good old days. The N.A. prohibited the meetings. But as they continued to be held, several of the ringleaders were arrested, tried, convicted and sentenced to six months' imprisonment. Others were deported. (In various colonies outside Africa, as well as in several East African countries, Governments have, on occasions such as this, tried to calm the public mind by prohibiting public meetings and the collecting of money, except by permission, that in Kenya has to be

POLITICS

got from the D.O., and in Tanganyika from the N.A. A friend with much legal experience informs the writer that it is doubtful whether on most of such occasions Governments do not overstep their powers. A deported person is a man who has been conducted by the police to a remote part of the country for an indeterminate period on the written instruction of the Governor, acting on sworn information, but without open trial. In Tanganyika a deportee is given 8d. a day to live on. But his wife and family, if they stay behind to keep home and garden going, have to fend for themselves.)

Still the agitation grew. The K.N.C.U. refused to buy the coffee of a local society that had elected an anti-N.A. committee. One Chagga chief killed one of his brothers, who had taken the popular side. For six months the Government refused to have him arrested—in the end he was tried and convicted—on the ground that the prestige of a chief must be supported. (This preposterous fallacy, that any good can come from hushing up crime committed by people in office, European or African, has been repeatedly exposed.) Some of the malcontents went to the most eminent firm of lawyers in the country, that had conducted the suit of the Masai chiefs over twenty years earlier, were advised that the Chagga rule was *ultra vires*, and filed a suit to put the matter to the test. The difficulties that both the clients and their counsel had to overcome were very great. Many of the former were deported, and money to pay the expenses of the latter had to be collected secretly. Though the court of first instance found that the Chagga rule was valid, the court of appeal decided it was *ultra vires*. But that was some time after things had come to a head.

By July 1937 so many of the best-respected Chagga had

been fined, imprisoned and deported, and both the Government and the N.A. were being so openly execrated, even by the women, that the local officials asked the acting-Governor to visit the District and address a baraza or formal gathering. He did so. He and his Swahili interpreter seems to have been the only speakers. The speech consisted partly of assurances that if the people would only stop their ears to wicked agitators, their all-wise Government would make them happy and prosperous, and partly of threats that the disobedient would be imprisoned, deported and in addition be punished in some new undisclosed manner. Nothing was said either to meet real grievances or to remove misconceptions. All that was, of course, pure irritation. But when he told his audience that the K.N.C.U. was their own, to make or mar, he made the people so furious that some sort of outbreak was certain. It would be pleasant, but unfair to readers, to ignore the fact that no small part of East African mis-government is due to the type of man who is chosen to govern. With few exceptions, the men who for the last thirty years have governed East African countries lived only with their social equals, and, having no first-hand knowledge of African life, reflected the ideas about it that were expressed in their own restricted circle. The reason, for example, that this man made a puerile speech to the Chagga, was that he supposed they had children's minds. And it is quite true that adults, of whatever race, who have had hardly any education, scholastic or other, do in some ways think and behave as children do. If this man had been able to overhear what people were saying about him and his speech, the shock might have opened his eyes. But that is just what such men never do.

Soon after this speech was delivered, the committee of

one of the local societies called a members' meeting. At that meeting, which was alleged to have been and no doubt was attended by everyone in the place, it was decided by acclamation to close the store belonging to the society, which was done. Next day the N.A. sent men to open it again, by forcing the lock. That night a mob, consisting no doubt of many other people besides the society's members, burned the store down. Troops were rushed to the spot by air from as far away as Nairobi. No resistance was offered them. An aeroplane displaying a machine gun flew low over the villages. Some 200 men were arrested, tried and convicted, though they protested that they had only done what the acting-Governor said they might—dispose as they pleased of their own property. Some seventy were either imprisoned or deported and the rest fined. The records of the trials show that while most of them gave coffee-growing as their occupation, some were school-teachers and artisans. Their names show that most were Christians. So far as is known, these men are still serving their sentences.

This Chagga trouble has been described in detail because only details can properly illumine. (Any reader who wishes further information should read Tanganyika Sessions Paper No. 2 of 1938, remembering, however, that it is an ex-parte statement of events.) On the main point, a careful study of all the information available has convinced the writer that the Government ought not to be blamed for resorting to compulsion when it did. Sir Donald Cameron, who in his time instructed N.A.s never to concern themselves with matters of trade, in his book roundly condemns his successor for using the Chagga N.A. to compel people to sell to the K.N.C.U. But one cannot see what else by that time there was to be done.

The false steps which, unless retracted, must lead to disaster, had been taken years before. True, the Chagga rule sharpened the dispute, and the silly speech of the acting Governor precipitated the disorder. But if there had been neither rule nor speech, and even if the price of coffee had stayed steady, disaster sooner or later was made certain by the withdrawal of the help that enthusiastic officials had given the K.N.P.A., and by the Government's deference to the European planters' refusal to enter a co-operative society that would have African members too. And these, the causes of the fatality, were not some one man's blunders, but deliberate acts of policy, for which the Colonial Office must take the responsibility.

This incident also raises the question how far an N.A. can represent both a tribe to the Government and a Government to the tribe. We may indeed add a third to the two causes of the disaster already fixed upon, and say that it could not have happened if the Chagga N.A. had represented the tribal opinion. Perhaps so. But how could an alien and autocratic Government possibly allow to exist local authorities that wanted to pursue a policy fundamentally at variance with its own? The incident also raises a deeper problem. In former times, when a chief proved unsatisfactory, he was got rid of. He might be killed. Or the leader of a rival faction might, with or without bloodshed, either replace him or secede and found another tribe. (There are plenty of similar events in our own history.) Oftenest of all perhaps, an unpopular chief would simply lose his authority, and be increasingly disregarded. People would take their disputes to some other man who was known to decide justly. African customary law was arbitral rather than penal. And as the duty of settling disputes was the main duty of a chief, and almost the sole mark of his office, and the fees that litigants paid him were almost his only revenue, the man whose decisions were acted on became in time the chief *de jure* as well as *de facto*.

Under a European Government no proceedings so irregular could be allowed. The chief takes his niche as a component part of the machinery of government. He is paid a salary and presented with robes, a staff, a signet ring, a chair of office—all foreign innovations. No other man's decision upon a case is legal or can be enforced, though it may be and often is acted upon. So the chief must not only be a fixture. He must also be given powers for which there is no traditional sanction, that make him in fact a petty monarch, secure from popular disapproval so long as he pleases the Government. Such is the process of calcification that must overtake chiefs and indirect rule under European Governments in existing conditions. It would be more correct to say " chiefs-in-council," for normally a chief is provided with a council. And here again there must be calcification. For formerly a council was not a fixed body but a panel of men who either attended voluntarily, or were called because considered the right men for the matter in hand. Popular election of members of council is rare, and often unsatisfactory, since, as no matters of principle are involved in elections, they are bound to turn on personal rivalries and faction.

One need revealed by the Chagga incident is for a travelling inspectorate under the Mandates Commission of the League of Nations, whose reports would be published. If in this case an inspector had been on the spot even so late as in 1931, publicity alone might have deflected the whole subsequent course of events.

It will be noted that there is nothing to suggest that even Sir Donald's N.A.s were destined to become integral units in a self-governing federation. Nor is there provision, either in their constitutions or in their functions, for those normal differences of opinion that elsewhere in the world divide the "right" from the "left." And Sir Donald makes no bones about the limits of their powers. They were to do exactly as he told them. One ought to admit that mainly traditional bodies are unlikely to show much intelligence, and that perhaps Sir Donald went as far as he ought to have. Yet movements of thought do already exist in East African tribes. The dowry system, with all its local variations, though not a purely African problem, is, for example, much disputed by Africans. Much cruelty results, despite official complacency, from the enforcement by the courts of the tribal law that compels a girl to live with the man with whose parents her parents had long before made a marriage contract. (Compulsion is not used in many tribes.) Many Africans would have this law changed. In fact the whole dowry system is here and there breaking down as the result of economic change. European opinion, on the contrary, is strongly opposed to any change in tribal customary law, in this matter of the dowry or any other. Formerly the law of a tribe responded automatically to a changed environment. That can still happen, but only so long as authority has not decided what the law of the tribe is. Once it has so decided, whatever the people of a tribe may wish, they are powerless to adapt their law to new conditions. Shepstone eighty years ago codified Zulu law as then existing. By now, Zulu have to go to European lawyers in Durban to have their own laws explained to them. The result is, not so much that forward-looking people

POLITICS

leave tribal society, for they would in any case, but that the tribe dies at the root.

The plain fact surely emerges, that in a time of so rapid change, no political adaptation that is suited to one generation can be expected to suit the next. Industrially, most people in East Africa, in Kenya nearly everyone, have undergone in two generations an industrial revolution that in Europe was spread over many centuries. By contrast, there has been hardly any deliberate political and social change. It must in any case take far longer to turn the tribesman into the citizen than to turn the peasant into the wage labourer. The great merit of the Cameron policy was that it was the first step forward in that harder process, as long a step perhaps, as was possible in face of the disbelief prevailing in high places. To call that policy an improvisation is no dispraise. Like the schools of the Christian Missions, it was an excellent makeshift, a temporary bridge constructed of traditional materials that, as did those schools, helped people over a gap that others were making no shift to cross. It bears all the marks of a makeshift. It assumes, for example, that European influence has gone so far as to convince people that sanitation is good, but not so far as to have given them the idea that good government is the concern of ordinary men and women. It assumes that the times demand some, but not too much, modification of the traditional. It assumes the directing hand of a disinterested autocrat, which Sir Donald no doubt was, but which is not a good definition of most African Governors. Above all, it assumes the persistence of tribalism. For it is vital to every variety of indirect rule that it must carry into the new age the loyalty that all gave instinctively in the old. And already tribal society is breaking up, far more rapidly in East than in West Africa. In every town, mining centre, sisal or other large estate, people of many tribes live together, amicably enough as a rule. Governments in East Africa do not even attempt as a rule to set up tribal jurisdictions in such places, that play a rapidly increasing part in African life. It is in the Gold Coast that the course of events proves how impossible it is to regard indirect rule as the final solution of any problem, even of African local government. Cocoa farmers in that country employ labourers from the far-off north, who in some cases come to be a majority of the population, urban and rural, of what once was a purely tribal area. In such places tribal jurisdiction, when disputes arise between farmers and their labourers, leaves the verdicts in the hands of courts that are composed of relatives of the farmers.

If readers now ask what the answers are to this series of conundrums, one can only say that the obviously right answer is also impossible. As things now are, people simply cannot decide for themselves. The idea that they might never enters anyone's head in Africa. If history is any guide, and it is the only one we have, African tribes will merge into nations. And if that process is to synchronize with the pace of the changes that we have forced on Africans' lives, it will be faster in tropical Africa than it ever has been anywhere else. Some suggestions on what Governments should and should not do in this difficult and confused situation are contained in the draft dispatch that is the last chapter in this book. If some readers deplore that in these pages the disappearance of tribal life is frankly anticipated, let them ask themselves if they do not thereby show that they too regard Africans as subhuman. Is it not as foolish and as unjust to deplore, and even try to prevent, the abandonment of tribal ideas and habits, as for parents to deplore and try to prevent their children's abandoning their toys and growing into men and women?

Before we leave this subject several prevalent fallacies must be noted. One hears people say that Africans ought to be careful to abandon only what is bad in their old ways of life. Who, one wonders, is to decide what is bad? The best way to judge this idea is for us to put ourselves in the place of ancestors of ours who were in a similar situation. In the eyes of the ardent reformer in seventeenth century Europe there was nothing good in feudalism. He left its virtues to be discovered centuries later, when no one was suffering from its faults. In any case ordinary Africans have no power to make deliberate choices, though there is much unconscious adaptation of life to the new circumstances that we have brought about because they suited or profited us.

Another fallacy is so patent as to seem unworthy of mention, yet is too widespread to be ignored. It is said that since, let us say, the Baganda were, sixty years ago, about as far on as our ancestors were a thousand years ago, it is likely to take them a thousand years to get to where we are now. But Africans now are "where" we are. Not only have they been forced into our industrial system. Inside that system they are deliberately restricted, in most East African countries, to the lowest place. Here we have no natural evolution. Distasteful though it may be, the only way to judge fallacies of this type by the relevant facts is to force ourselves to answer the question we began by asking, whether Africans have or have not ordinary human natures and capacities. If they have, then to postpone social development and liberation in Africa to a distant future is to force on African children

THE COLOUR BAR IN EAST AFRICA

now at school, who have the capacities that our children have, artificial participation in a life that only ignorance enables them to tolerate.

Some account must also be given of what is not so much a fallacy as a false standpoint. This illustrated outline of British East African affairs differs from other books on the subject by being based on the belief that one day ordinary Africans will be sovereign, that therefore what matter most are the forces that are forming their minds and habits, and that the one thing our country must decide is whether to help them on or to continue to hold them back. Many people take an opposite point of view. For them the primary aspect of African affairs is their relation with Europe and America, the importance of the continent as the source of certain raw materials, and the strategic as well as the economic values that accrue to European nations from their possession of its tropical parts. No space need be wasted in proving that the rivalry of jealous European States is never likely even to be alleviated by treating Africa as a cake, of which the biggest slices go to the nations with the biggest knives. What does deserve examination is the general conception that makes people adopt this standpoint. When the affairs of any ordinary country, Canada, let us say, or Spain, are in question, we assume that the interests of Canadians or Spaniards are the sole consideration. Even when such facts are considered as that Canada provides the world with most of its nickel, or Spain with much of its cork or mercury, we never dream of interfering with how or to whom those raw materials are sold, and in fact expect Canadians and Spaniards to get the highest prices they can for them from each customer in turn. Why is it that so many people regard African countries so differently? There can be no doubt of the answer. It is because they regard African countries as possessions, as belonging to European nations, not to their inhabitants. And the reason at the bottom of their minds for their thinking in that way is that they assume that the wrong answer to the question we started with is the true one.

But, some will object, even if all that is true, it is beside the point. Such people's ideas may be as wrong as you say they are, and you may be right about the reason for their false thinking. Yet the fact remains that their ideas, not yours, are being acted upon. Their coinage may be spurious, but it is accepted in the world's markets, which is what really matters. Africa after all is treated as a cake, from which certain people do carve slices for their own consumption. And as long as they do so, other people with no cake will continue, as they have opportunity, to see whose knives are the sharpest. Only too true. So let us examine this cake as closely as we can, and see what it consists of.

It is true, though not very important, that as citizens the people of this country are losers rather than gainers from their " possessions." Nyasaland, for example, costs us over £100,000 a year. The point is hardly relevant. The cake is the money that only the few of us get, as we have seen them do, in Rhodesia out of copper, and in Nyasaland out of tobacco. Prestige of course does count too. But it is not the operative factor. The people of any European country only begin to want an empire when some few of them hope to make much money as a result. That is historically true. It narrows the problem, the international problem that arises from the fact that wealth produced in Africa is disposed of on a different principle from the one that we saw is followed in Canada and Spain.

The only kind of transference from the "haves" that would be of any use to the "have-nots" consists of shares in companies with investments in Africa, and of the money they pay in royalties and salaries. So here we come to the ultimate facts. If people are serious when they insist that "realism" demands of us this international view of African affairs, they must address themselves to the practical questions, whose wealth is to be surrendered, and what proportion of it, and, to whom it is to be transferred. The writer knows of no answers to those questions that make sense. He sees no reason why shareholders in Rhodesian copper mines should be mulcted more than or rather than shareholders in Welsh coal mines. Nor does he see any reason, even in an ideally pacific world, for making presents from the wealth produced in Africa, to German or Italian capitalists. He is therefore forced to conclude that those realists do not themselves think realistically. They cannot have tried to formulate their ideas in terms of fact. There is good reason of course for treating Europe and Africa inter-dependently. But to treat African countries as possessions, the policy to be pursued in which ought to be dependent on the needs of European countries, is both unreasonable and sure to result in wars. The true realists therefore are those who would have our country take the only course that can prevent African countries from being pawns in the game of power politics, which is at once to undertake the preparation of their inhabitants for self-government.

We would do well to enquire why it is that people in general have been so misled in this matter. We all know that money counts. It has a dead-weight drag on politics. But normally it is counteracted. Shareholders in African ventures are not specially wicked people. They do not bribe the Press or pay men to write falsehoods in books. How is it then that this East African policy continues? It certainly would not, if the facts were generally known. One has only to lay such facts as those about Rhodesian copper before people casually met, in village inns, in trains, anywhere. Most of them will refuse to believe you. But if they must believe, because they know you, they will not mince matters. They will call a Government that allows mining companies to pay, in dividends of from 20 per cent. to 80 per cent., twenty times as much as they pay to 17,000 miners, the kind of names that trustees are called only when they find themselves in the dock. This question of responsibility is of primary importance. There can be no political change without the exercise of forces at the right place. Who then in this case can use the motive forces? The preceding pages have failed to explain the situation if readers think it fair either to blame the people whom we may call the contending parties, the several million Africans and the several thousand European immigrants and financiers, or to expect from either of them the forces needed to bring about reform. Neither, in point of fact, had the responsibility of bringing about the existing situation. Are we then to expect action from the men, in Downing Street and Africa, who have inherited the situation, for the men who created it are dead or in retirement? Most certainly not. They are the servants, not the masters, of the public, and it is not for them to overturn or to condemn the work of their predecessors. On those predecessors a truly heavy burden of responsibility rests, that now will never be lifted. Even if they were only obeying orders, which was not always the case, as in the instance of the Masai, they knew that they had only to protest, sometimes only to explain, to prevent the wrongs from being done.

That chapter of Imperial history is closed. Who then are the men who are responsible for what is being done to-day, that will be history to-morrow? In our democracy, the British electorate. That electorate expects to be informed and is informed. Professor Macmillan and others have written truthfully about South African affairs, which, however, are no longer our business. But in the many books that have recently been published that deal with East Africa, some in seats of learning, by men and women endowed with chairs and out of trust funds, only the fringe of the truth at best is lifted. It is to such men of position and influence, who often admit in private what their readers could never suspect, that the public rightly looks for the truth. Their silence is the reason why the wrongs are not righted.

CHAPTER X

EDUCATION

DURING the long struggle for the abolition, first of the trade in slaves and finally of chattel slavery itself, most of the Bishops in the House of Lords condoned and defended both. Except for the Friends, the Independents and a Presbyterian sect in Scotland, that was the part the Churches played, not only in that controversy, but also in the one over child labour and in many others that were moral as well as political issues. In our own time, so long as the Covenant of the League and collective security were popular the Churches joined in the chorus of their supporters. But when that chorus fell silent, its clerical supporters, with few exceptions, fell silent too. That is why many of us are anti-clerical. Conscience forbids us to accept as guides bodies that take the wrong side at least as often as the right in conflicts of opinion, while their outcome is in doubt. If the label on a bottle is not even presumptive evidence of the nature of its contents, we say the right place for it is the dustbin. That is not the case of the Christian Missions that overspread Africa in the nineteenth century. They were not in the least like the churches we know. As the part they played in Africa was vitally important, we must try to understand it. The account of it that follows will be written in the past tense, for two reasons. It is many years now since the writer spent some days or weeks on some score of Mission stations. And since he left Africa there is evidence that Missions are growing more like Churches.

The people who, mainly in Britain and America, sent missionaries to Africa, did intend them to convert the heathen. It was what men and women found after they arrived in Africa that transformed their aim. What so affected them was not so much the obvious fact that people's morals in Africa were no worse than in Christendom—in some respects were better. Some were no doubt influenced by the discovery that on the only authentic occasion on which Jesus referred to making proselytes it was to condemn the practice. But what made Missions what they were was the need of help they found that Africans had. As they got to know the people they learned how they suffered from diseases, poverty, superstition and ignorance. Thousands of men and women, many of them highly educated, became *servi servorum*.

All of us know of people who devote their lives to others, oftenest but by no means always, from marital or parental relationship. But this was no mere personal affair. Several million pounds a year were spent by Missions, mainly on schools and hospitals. In Nyasaland, for example, a third of the children in the country were in Mission schools by 1914, while all that the Government did was to give them a subsidy of £3,000. Missions also taught people how to burn and build with bricks, the use of wheels for transport, and a host of other arts and trades. They introduced coffee and cocoa, as well as fruit trees, cattle and poultry to tribes to which they had been unknown. And all this wide range of services was done, not by men at desks and in offices, but by men and women working alongside Africans, whose aim was simply to serve, and to give, out of their vastly greater opportunities of learning, all that they had to give, without stint or measure.

There have been movements in history akin to this. There have been times when some multitude unites to pursue a life of self-sacrifice in a cause so splendid as to make it infinitely desirable. That was how the early Franciscans felt and acted. All such movements are entered by people who have no real vocation for them, by people who believe they ought to join them but are not happy in them. And from various causes all such movements become respectable, and die. It would be unreasonable to hope that this movement, that has had so great results in Asia as well as Africa, should follow any different course. Historians tell us it was the evangelical revival that made England sober and industrious. It also gave to millions of Africans their only inkling of a way of life at variance with the one described in these pages. In Europe we believe that Governments give children a better education than Churches give. But in Africa, as we have seen, Governments have no intention of making their subjects free citizens and hence cannot be expected to give the children of those subjects a liberal education.

When, in some countries just before, in others just after, the Great War, East African Governments first set up Education Departments, they had to decide what policy to adopt to the already long-established Mission schools. The defects of those schools were notorious. What their critics then and now habitually forget is that they were infinitely better than nothing and that precisely nothing was what the other participants in African affairs, including Governments, did until forced into some sort of action by opinion at home. In no one of the six countries in British East Africa do as many as 3 per cent. of the children attend Government schools now in 1940 : in two of them there are no Government schools for African children at all. But what is supremely important, and supremely difficult, is to perpetuate, under the direction of Governments, the spirit of enthusiastic devotion that made happy oases of many Mission stations when they were independent. In those days it was common for African teachers to refuse offers from Governments and employers of twice the wages Missions gave them. By contrast, in the mental atmosphere prevailing in European circles, Governments at first found it almost impossible to find European teaching staffs. In several countries ex-missionaries were appointed to the more responsible posts. (Missions pay salaries far lower than people with the same qualifications get at home and it was no discredit to some of them that when money had to be found for their children's education they accepted the far larger salaries Government offered them.) By this time, no doubt, there are men and women teaching in Government schools who have the same enthusiasm for their work as is common in England. But great dangers must beset State education in Africa until British policy is given a different general aim. Those dangers can best be seen in quotations from the hitherto unpublished report of an inspector whom the Colonial Office sent fourteen years ago to report on education in Nigeria.

From most of Northern Nigeria, with some nine million inhabitants, nearly half of them Moslem, Christian Missions then were and still are excluded. The Government had, accordingly, a free hand, and for twenty years, when this report was written, had been giving the country the schools, the staff and the educational policy it considered the best. In Southern Nigeria, on the other hand,

EDUCATION

as elsewhere in British Africa, education was and is the joint concern of Government and Missions.

This inspector found that only 2,409 boys were in Government schools in Northern Nigeria. (About the same number went to schools belonging to the severely restricted Missions.) Of the 2,409, 330 were in trade schools and of the rest, there were in :

Standard I	1,004	Standard IV	182
Standard II	450	Standard V	84
Standard III	333	Standard VI	26

The experience of every country is that most children whose education stops at Standard I and many of those who fail to reach Standard III later forget how to read and count. The inspector commented : " There were no girls being educated and the Director told me there was no thought of Government educating girls." Of conditions in Southern Nigeria he noted that there were 634 girls in Government and 8,727 in Mission schools, and adds, " Even so there are four boys being educated to every girl. This is serious. It means a large proportion of ignorant homes in the next generation. Economically the education of a girl is worth more than the education of a boy. It means healthier homes and children. Where the father alone is educated he does not pass on much as a rule to his children, for the obscurantist wife dominates inside the home the educated man. Girls' education is also of vital political importance. Educated men who cannot find any but ignorant wives are restless and discontented and are apt to stand loose from their tribes." [1]

[1] The education of girls, like women's rights in general, is most backward in Moslem countries, except where, as in Turkey, what is misleadingly called Western civilization is the aim of the Government. In British Africa as a whole, about half as many girls as boys get elementary education.

He wrote of one Government school:

" The Munchi are a naked people, but in school have to be clothed. The clothing decided on is akin to Hausa dress. The Munchi staff asked for an interview with the Director during my visit: it was to petition him to allow them to wear shorts and shirts. This was promptly refused. The point is that if you are training leaders of a people you must not treat them as the children they may be, but as the reasonable thinkers you expect them to become. I am not here arguing either for shorts or for Hausa wear, for a Western or an Arabian background for Pagans. The point is that educationally it is impossible to train a staff who are treated (and thought of) as babes who have no right to guide themselves at all. It is this attitude behind all the Government of the North that explains much of the stagnation."

The Director of Education frankly admitted to the inspector that the schools he directed were unpopular, though in Moslem districts, where nearly all the schools were, a mosque stood in every school compound. The chief reason why in many parts, though not all, Government schools were much less popular than Mission schools was that in the former the staff were sahibs and in the latter servants, who, moreover, were despised by their fellow-countrymen for attempting to behave to Africans as other than their masters. How difficult the co-operation of people of types so different must be can easily be imagined.

Further, the inspector's report illustrates how expensive Government education in Africa is apt to be. He gave the cost per pupil as over £30 in Northern Nigeria. In Southern Nigeria the annual cost to Government per pupil in State schools was £3 15s. and in Mission schools 23s. In the Gold Coast the figures were £6 4s. in Government and 26s. in Mission schools. Except in the case of

EDUCATION

Northern Nigeria, those are representative figures for British Africa generally. And it may be added that at a rough general estimate, of the cost of education in Mission schools, about a third or rather more is borne by Governments, another third by Mission funds, and the rest by parents' fees and local levies. Even more significant are the proportions of their total revenues that Governments spend on education. (The facts are fully given in Lord Hailey's *Survey*.) So long ago as in 1919 18 per cent. of the revenue of the Philippines was spent on education. In no country in our Colonial Empire is the proportion as high as 5 per cent. In the countries of British East and British West Africa it lies between 1·5 per cent. and 3 per cent.

On educational policy generally the inspector already quoted wrote :

"In the early days the first need of administrators was to find clerks, interpreters and subordinate workers for Government and commercial houses. But when even a small proportion of the children of a country had been educated, they not only supplied that need but overflowed to become a stagnant and possibly dangerous flood with no adequate outlet. While individual schools here and there may usefully aim at vocational training, there is much more harm than good to be expected from any *system* which aims at supplying any narrower need than that of the country as a whole, and that must always be chiefly Africans' need of Africans for African work and life."

And his pregnant and pungent verdict on the men then responsible for Government policy in Northern Nigeria was that they had " no outlook beyond the present and little beyond the past." Except in Achimota in the Gold Coast and, it is to be hoped, in the college in Uganda now being founded, the narrow vocational policy, whereby education is restricted to what fits youth for posts known to be open to them, is still accepted by the authorities in British Africa generally.

Some arrangement between Governments and Missions is obviously a necessity in existing conditions. This is not the place to discuss what arrangement is the best. But there is one matter that might be put right by ventilation. Africa of course is not the only place where some men tell others how to do work they could not do themselves. But this subject of popular education is so supremely important that it should be recognized that Directors and Inspectors and Supervisors ought never to direct or inspect work unless they have done it themselves. A personal experience of the writer's may be allowed. He once volunteered to teach English in a night school to aspiring dock labourers. He completely failed. He knew the men's language well enough. It was just that he found that teaching them English was a difficult art, like drawing a portrait or walking a tightrope, for which his mental equipment was inadequate. In the end he found he could just manage to explain to the lowest class that the signs b-a meant the sound ba.

Readers who have themselves taught may care to know the main facts about contemporary education in Kenya, taken from the annual report for 1938. The local nomenclature is confusing, so that the three kinds of school, sub-elementary, elementary and primary are not what they seem. A sub-elementary school is a village chapel, costing perhaps £5 at most to build, in which children are taught to pray and sing as well as to read, write and count, by a man getting little more than a labourer's wage, who supports himself mainly by cultivating the soil, as all his neighbours do. In sub-elementary schools

EDUCATION

children are taught what our children learn in their first standard, and most of the 150,000 children who in Kenya get any education at all never get beyond them. Of them the report says " very few of these schools obtain grants because the elementary schools in the next grade absorb all the available funds." And, rather surprisingly, the Director adds, " more than half the literate Africans learned to read in sub-elementaries." Their cost is met out of Mission funds, parents' fees and local levies.

Next come the elementary schools, attended by 40,000 boys and 17,000 girls. In them in theory, and in most of them in practice, children are given a five-year course that takes them as far as Standard III. The report adds that " a few reach Standard IV in a sixth year and in selected schools simple English is taught in the fifth and sixth years." It observes that " children who have completed Standard I in a sub-elementary school will walk long distances to attend the top classes in an elementary school." Of the 57,000 children in elementary schools 5,002 are in Government schools and a few hundred in schools built and maintained by the Kikuyu N.A., despite natural though discreditable discouragement from Government and Missions. The rest are in Mission schools that are chapels too. The cost of building them is as a rule partly met by a grant of £50 from the Government, that is spent on equipment and galvanized roofing. Their annual cost, that is salaries and maintenance, was until 1938 met in roughly equal proportions by the Government, out of Mission funds, and from local tribal rates (over £18,000) and parents' fees (over £9,000). The Government insists on fees being charged, that vary from 6d. a term to a pound or more, in all State and aided schools. And though the fact was disputed in a Parliamentary answer, many thousands of children are expelled from schools because their parents will not or cannot pay their fees. (The writer has long lists of the names of such schools, parents and children.) In 1938 the Government stopped its subsidies to those Mission schools, and thus threw all their cost on Missions, parents' fees and the taxes levied by N.A.s. The reason it gave was that the money is better spent on the favoured few who get some more costly education. The total cost of running Mission schools averages a little more than £2 per pupil per year. In all Government schools for Africans it averages over £6.

About 9,000 African children and youths in Kenya attend schools higher or other than elementary. The majority are in "primary" schools that are boarding schools, most of which belong to Missions, in which the training of teachers is the main object. The report says "competition for admission to primary schools is very keen." The Africans who get by far the most expensive education in Kenya are in the "native industrial training depot" that cost in 1938 £11,769 or £29 16s. per apprentice. All those trained in the depot are of course destined for European employment. The report says "there are four aided Mission schools giving secondary education, 213 pupils in the junior and 18 in the senior forms." There is no Government secondary school for Africans in Kenya. But 55 youths from Kenya have bursaries to study at Makerere College in Uganda, and two are studying in Britain at a cost to Government of £300.

Altogether the Government spent in 1938 on African education £80,284, of which £53,494 went in subsidies to Missions. That works out at about 12s. per registered child and about 4s. 3d. per child of school age. Of the

EDUCATION

9,389 Indian children at school in Kenya the Government spends £43,861 or about £5 a head.

The report is far from clear as to how the cost of educating European children is met. There are 1,160 of them in Government schools, most of them boarders, and nearly as many in private schools. The cost of " European education " is given as £49,000 and of tuition only the gross cost per pupil is said to be £27 12s. and the net cost £23 13s., fees presumably accounting for the difference. The corresponding figures for Africans are £4 10s. and £4 6s. Of Government boarding schools for Europeans the report says " the total amount of fees paid was 55 per cent. of the sum represented by the full fees." And in another passage it says that of the pupils in those same schools 12 per cent. are " wholly free " and 51·7 per cent. " partly free." It thus appears that most European parents in Kenya not only escape paying direct taxation, except for the trifling poll tax, but get most of the cost of their children's education paid for them out of State funds. African parents, by contrast, go to jail for a month if they cannot pay their direct taxation, and, after they have paid their hut and poll tax and their local rates, that Europeans escape paying altogether, if they cannot pay school fees in addition, they see their children expelled from school. In other words, the education of the children of the richest people in the country is subsidized out of the taxes paid by the poorest, whose own children get no education at all. The authorities would indignantly deny that interpretation of the facts. Readers can judge those facts for themselves.

Comment would be otiose on this the greatest and worst of the East African colour bars. It achieves absurdity as well as notoriety. For there are separate schools, with separate curricula, not only for Africans, Indians and Europeans, but for Arabs and Goans too. The author's proposals for dealing with the situation described above are contained in the last chapter of this book.

The early travellers tell us that chiefs hoed in their food gardens like other people, perhaps wearing a leopard instead of a goat skin. Now, though colour bars set a limit to what can be reached, East Africans everywhere imitate our hierarchy of Mammon. Already the gulf between the clerk or even the lorry driver with ten or twenty pounds a year and the labourer with two or three is as wide as between cabin and steerage passengers in our ships. This upstart middle class is recruited from industry and from Missions. There have been sporadic movements of protest in East Africa. Quite unorganized, and soon stifled, news of few of them, if any, has reached our newspapers. In every case the protesters have been men who had been taught in Mission schools, despite the fact that in most of them loyalty is taught of a type that most of us regard as odious. It is difficult for people in this country to imagine how ignorant of politics and economics the men belonging to this relatively fortunate minority in East Africa are, some of them literate, others semi-skilled in some manual trade. They do read Reuter in local papers, and so have some knowledge of world events. They were angry about Abyssinia, especially when Mr. Chamberlain courted Mussolini. But they cannot rid themselves of the delusion that our society is a replica of their own. Thus they suppose that King George governs as well as reigns and not only appoints the man of his personal choice to every position of authority, but also disposes of every acre of land in England. If we bear in mind that hardly any people in East Africa have been taught what all our children learn and that from all the six countries not fifty men have spent a month or more in England, such misconceptions will seem less strange. And after all, how many Englishmen understand what are the essential differences between East African society and their own ? Also it may be doubted if those who govern in Africa wish the people to learn that authority with us rests with a popularly elected Parliament and that most people in England have to work with their hands quite as hard as Africans do.

Such demands as this educated minority makes seem to us selfish. Men with incomes of £10 or £20 fail, for example, to see that the tax must be a far heavier burden to the much poorer majority than to themselves. Educated East Africans are often on bad terms with their N.A.s and as a class are intensely disliked by Europeans. They are doubly unhappy in having left, of their own accord, their own society for ours, and yet in finding, in our society, only the slipperiest of footholds. The few small organized groups that have grown up in Nyasaland and the large Kavirondo Tax Payers Association are no more than mutual improvement societies. And the Kikuyu Central Association is rent by faction and has more than once been wrecked by dishonest office bearers. Partly because there is nothing like a trade union among Europeans for them to copy, partly because those with some education fail to make common cause with their fellows, partly because a strike, being a breach of contract, is a criminal offence, no industrial organization exists.

One of the bad results of the partnership in education between Governments and Missions is the decay of the mutual confidence that used to prevail between missionaries and those they had taught. The old-style missionary tended to be indiscriminate in what he taught. In many a village court-yard in Nyasaland Roman and Presbyterian would go hammer and tongs over the merits and demerits of the Protestant Reformation. But now all must work to a code, or do without grants in aid. And the code restricts the education African children get to what our children learn by the time they are ten, to training in certain clerical and manual occupations, and, in some schools, to instruction in English. People used to distinguish missionaries from other Europeans. No one denies that Africans get some benefit from the activities of officials who go to Africa to earn their salaries, of merchants who go to buy and sell at a profit, of settlers and mine managers who go to extract from African soil an income from their capital higher than they could get at home. But the benefit is incidental. And where, in East Africa, it is widest spread, it is paid for. Colour bars are part of the price. And in the last war a larger proportion of the population of Tanganyika and Kenya lost their lives than the proportion of the people of this island who did.[1]

[1] A much valued critic writes of this passage: " I do think this plainly unjust. It is not true of men I know well in Government service, in educational and political services, who have the true missionary spirit." That is perfectly true. There are public servants in every country who transcend their duties, at much cost to themselves and sometimes to the detriment of their prospects. There are men and women in England, for example, who feed children whom it is their duty only to teach. There are employers of labour who befriend the men they employ. To take an extreme case, there are no doubt Nazi storm troopers who protect Jews whom it is their official duty to persecute. There are two ways of judging these matters. If we look at them from above we shall judge how far Governments, local and national, make it easy for men in authority to be the friends and servants of those with whom they have official relations. In the case of East Africa, readers must decide that question for themselves. But if we look at these matters from below, we must accept, in our case of East Africa, the standpoint that in fact Africans take. And they do regard all officials with mistrust and suspicion, however kind some of them may be, since they are parts of the machinery of Government. Devoted missionaries too, these days, as well as devoted officials, find people ungrateful.

EDUCATION

Life in East Africa is less sombre than the recital of bare industrial and political facts would suggest. But these facts should at least make plain why friendship with Africans in Africa is possible only to Europeans who live in Africa with some other end in view than profit. One remembers such a man. He went about all day with a sort of retinue. There would be a deputation from a far-off village that wanted a school : a man from some other village wanted him to go to someone whom a leopard had mauled: a carpenter demanded his attention to a door he couldn't get to fit or to the mending of the station's only surviving hurricane lamp: schoolboys would insist on the inflation of an already often-burst football. No wonder the inspection of schools in the district was neglected and that even on the station classes were irregular if not haphazard. No meal was uninterrupted, and even in the evenings conversation was difficult. Small boys from the boarding school would flit into the room, lit only by a candle, and squat under tables and chairs. Driven out to bed—on wooden trestles—they would flit back again, their bare feet noiseless on the floor of beaten mud. On Sundays all crowded into the church of strange shape, the walls certainly never parallel, the bricks of many shapes and colours. Of the congregation, a few proudly wore cast-off clothes from Europe that then were largely imported into Africa, most prized of all the red coats of the old British Army, though even a pair of old stays might serve for Sunday best. From the unglazed windows floated howls rather than song and with them the smell of sweat and of the rancid fat worn by the less fashionable majority, that mingled with the smell of the goats tethered at the church door, which, together with fowls suspended by their feet, corncobs and baskets of grain, flour and pulse, made up the church collection. It all seemed somehow to fit the old African scene, and was, in fact the only kind of European invasion that people could, and did, adapt to their needs and wishes, and so welcome as their own. In these more seemly times, schools are ruled, quite rightly of course, by the syllabus, with a dreaded examination the test, for teacher and taught, of success. But one hopes that in the remoter parts of Africa the old warmth and the old liberty may still survive.

Addendum

In August 1940 Mr. Creech Jones was informed in Parliament by Mr. George Hall, the Under-Secretary of State, that two other local bodies as well as the Kikuyu Central Association had been declared by the Governor of Kenya to be "societies dangerous to the good government of the Colony." Asked what evidence existed in support of that view, Mr. Hall said that "a report is awaited from the Governor." It is probable that these three societies are the only ones in the country that are really indigenous and representative of the educated minority in Kenya. And it is more than probable that their declared aims and actual activities would in this country be regarded, not only as harmless but also as eminently praiseworthy.

CHAPTER XI

THE BACKGROUND

WE think now of Austrians as a cultured, gay, pleasure-loving people. That was not the picture our grandfathers had of them. So brutal and domineering used they to be thought that when an Austrian general unwisely visited London he was mobbed by brewers' draymen—in Brussels he was nearly killed. Then, Northern Italy was an Austrian Dependency. Now, Austria is a German Dependency. How can a country rightly be said to have a national character when in so short a time it displays not only different but contradictory characteristics ? The Italians too are in the same case. No modern Democrat hates Fascism so fiercely as Mazzini and Garibaldi would have hated it. Undoubtedly the Italy that those two men inspired was the real Italy. Now the real Italy is proud of having subjugated Ethiopians and Albanians, and tramples on liberty within her own borders as it was never trampled on by the oncehated Austria. Which then of those two faces shows the true national character of Italy ? Nor are we ourselves in any different case. Thirty years ago Britain and Russia treated Persia as a cake, but were so slow with their knives that the Great War overtook them before they swallowed a crumb. And Germany ? However hard to believe it may be, it is yet true that until Bismarck's time no country in Europe was so easy-going and so unambitious. We each may choose from a score of cases of the kind abundant evidence to prove the falsity of the belief that the people of any country differ in any important respect from the people of other countries. Clearly there can be no such thing as a permanent national character. What is believed to be a country's national character gets its features from the character of the men who control it and represent it to the outer world. In every country there are men and women with types of character as different as Mazzini and Mussolini, Gladstone and Rhodes. There are, and must be in every generation, some lovers of liberty, for all mankind as for themselves, and some who love to subdue, to dominate and to enslave. In every period of recorded time there have been cases closely resembling those we have just noted, the Austrian treatment of Italians, the Italians' treatment of Albanians, the treatment Britain and Russia meant to give the Persians.

It should be carefully noted that cruelty is not the essential thing, although it obviously is far easier for a man to be cruel to people under him than to people who are on his level. The essential thing is not the floggings inside concentration camps, but the camps themselves, the bare fact that men and women are shut up for having opinions or convictions of their own, or for having Jewish parents. There are concentration camps building in the minds of some people in every country. But in civilized countries, where the laws give equal rights to all, those natural bullies cannot find vent for their brutality on any scale. Cruelty is prevented, not mainly by punishing those who commit cruel acts, but by denying people the power of domination over other people's lives, and so leaving them hardly a chance to be cruel. The source of domination is pride, the pleasure some people have in looking down on other people, and in feeling that they are in their power. Pride can exist alone. Concentration camps bring no profit to Herr Hitler. But when pride is conjoined with desire of gain, with the ambition to profit by power over the lives of others, the kind of domination resulting is the basest and foulest.

Every normal society protects its members from this vice, which is an ineradicable part of human nature. Hence the instinct to dominate is forced to find new outlets, and these in turn are blocked. That is why constant vigilance is necessary, since in each age new outlets are found that in an unvigilant society result in evils that people had fondly supposed they had finally cured. A new outlet is naturally never given a name already in use for some former manifestation of the vicious instinct. That is one reason why the public mind is confused over this vital issue. Looking back over the centuries, it is hard to believe that our forefathers could have imagined, a century ago, that by abolishing chattel slavery they had made an end of an ineradicable instinct, which, in every age since the dawn of history, had shown itself in diverse institutional forms. Abolition nevertheless was no small achievement. The abolitionists not only blocked the outlet that for centuries had made domination easy, but for the first time in history branded the thing itself. They did even more. By insisting on equal rights for all, chattel slave and owner alike, they made the devising of new forms of slavery almost impossible.

But equal rights, as we have seen, have gone by the board in East Africa. The gains of a century ago have been lost, except that everywhere in the Empire, and nearly everywhere in the world, it is no longer possible for one man to own another man's body. The truly strange thing is that this long backward step was taken by the generation that was the first clearly to lay bare that other root of domination and enslavement, the economic. Many readers, who believe that profit is the motive from which spring all the wrongs that man does to man, will have been astonished to find that their forefathers were so simple as to imagine that those wrongs could be righted by so purely political a remedy as mere equality before the law. Yet we should not have needed a Hitler to prove to us that human injustice has a root that goes deeper into our natures than any economic analysis can reveal. None would deny that there are economic causes of injustice in Africa. We can with reason go further, and say that Capitalism in Africa, since there is no one to tame it as, under democratic government, it has been tamed, is seen at its worst. But to say that Emancipation was a political measure is no criticism of the Emancipators. Even if those economists are right who say that profits have been made from free labour that could not have been made from slave labour, yet was the step the Emancipators took the right one to take first. They struck at power. They closed for ever, we hope, one outlet for the vicious instinct to dominate and enslave.

What then happened was bound to happen. Men set themselves, after a little delay, to devise new ways of getting men into their power. As it was their instinct that moved them, they did not fully recognize either their motive or the purpose of the specific measures they took. They acted in fulfilment of their sense of power over other people's lives, though when to that the desire of gain was added, they behaved with more conscious deliberation. What measures, accordingly, would men so moved to act be expected to take, on the sole condition that, in consequence of Emancipation, no person was to be allowed to use direct compulsion upon another? For some fifty years after Emancipation, we saw that there was another condition, namely, that the laws must not discriminate between a country's inhabitants, on the ground of their race or religion. But that condition, as we also saw, has in East Africa been tacitly abandoned.

Let us ask the question in more precise terms. What in an uncivilized country with over three million inhabitants would some 20,000 people from a civilized country do, in order to get power over the lives of the 3,000,000, and to gain wealth from the exercise of their power? First, they would take as much political power as their country would allow them. A franchise law that discriminated, so as to give every single one of them the vote and to refuse it to every one of the three millions, would be very useful for that purpose. Second, they would induce the Government to take possession of all the land in the country, give back to the three millions what they needed for self-support, and give them what was worth having of the rest. Third, they would concert with the Government measures that would enable standard wage rates to be fixed high enough to enable the three million to pay as much as possible of the revenue from taxes, but no higher, so that as far as possible they would escape taxation themselves. Fourth, they would get the Government to make laws that gave it power to shut any school it pleased, and stop any man it pleased from teaching, to restrict what the children of the three million were taught to matters that suited them, to the exclusion of matters that might excite interest in and result in protests against their situation. Fifth and last, they would inculcate among their countrymen at home the belief that the three millions belonged to a race that lacked the full human endowment. And these, together with many other subsidiary measures, are precisely what our countrymen resident in the Rhodesias, as well as in Kenya, have done. When looked at from the angle we chose, when we enquired what a civilized minority would do in order to get power, those five measures seem to be a coherent and consciously designed programme. But in fact they were not. As we saw, neither the hut tax, for example, nor the acquisition of the whole of the land, was anything more than the shortest way out of an urgent practical difficulty. As time went on, no doubt, measures were more and more deliberately adapted to the exercise of power. But at no time did most of the men who, either as Governors or as settlers, took those measures, say to themselves what can we do to increase, stabilize or complete our power. We may call the few who probably did bad men if we like. The majority were certainly not bad men. And that is what makes of supreme importance the fact that Europeans in East Africa took the last of those five measures in good faith. They are entirely convinced that Africans do not have natures and capacities the same as their own. If they gave the question to which we keep returning its true answer—even if they had any doubt about Africans' inherent inferiority, peace of mind would be impossible to them.[1]

[1] One of the friends who read the type-script of this book writes that this passage " gives the impression that the desire to dominate and cruelty are in some way ' natural ' and inevitable, and that if they do not come out in one way they will in another." Cruelty aside, one would answer that most people lack opportunity to dominate others, except in the family, where the vice is fairly common. But also that when opportunity does arise, the instinct to dominate, like the related though distinct acquisitive instinct, does " come out " unless controlled, as do all our instincts, for

We may note that the only Empire of the past that so satisfied its subjects for centuries that they believed it to be eternal was the Roman. There were periods in its history when corruption and rapacity induced disaffection and even revolt. But we should observe what it was that during most of that age submerged men's natural patriotisms in a common loyalty to Rome. Unquestionably it was the extension, for a relatively small fee, of equal rights with native-born Romans, at first to other Italians, and later to all Roman subjects. Not, of course, political rights, since they could in practice be exercised only by residents in Rome, but what then were more prized and what now are still quite as important, civil rights, the right to own land, to engage in trade, to join those guilds, the members of which alone could practise the learned professions and engage in skilled trades, and, most significant of all perhaps, the right to enter the civil and

which we are indebted to our animal ancestry. The avidity with which many people seized on the doctrines of Sigmund Freud, in themselves at best imperfectly proved, and the still more doubtful interpretation they put upon them, showed how "natural" it is to believe that the control of our instincts is injurious and wrong. What kinds of control are wise and right is a matter of controversy. But few people would deny that the acquisitive instinct is properly controlled by laws against theft and fraud. And few readers, it is hoped, will deny that laws enforcing equality of status for all ought in East Africa to hold in check the instinct that tempts some to dominate others. Admittedly laws are not enough. Besides stigmatizing domination as infamous, society ought to educate us to make personal efforts to embrace a way of life in which the maximum of personal liberty is combined with the maximum advantage to and liberty of others. Without such efforts, civilization would be replaced by anarchy. This positive aim must of course be an ideal only partially attainable. It may be recalled how one authority was asked to define who he meant by the neighbour, whom, he had said, one ought to love as oneself. In answer he instanced the case of a man who was (*a*) a foreigner, (*b*) with a wrong sort of religion, who was (*c*) in need, and (*d*) in sight. In other words, all such relations as one may have with all one's fellows ought at all times to be completely fraternal. The theory behind that ideal is that its pursuit results in more happiness than does obedience to one's natural instincts, among them the instinct to dominate.

military services, and to rise in them by merit to any rank, so that one of the ablest of the Emperors was not ashamed of being the grandson of a slave. When Indian coolies and Kikuyu labourers can hope that ability in their grandsons may be as well rewarded, we shall have reason to have confidence in the permanence of the British Empire.

We have now, it is hoped, seen evidence enough to be convinced that the first thing to be done in East Africa is to make all a country's inhabitants equal before the law. That must be done first, because you can do nothing with men who are half-slave and half-free. They have no inner sense of propulsion. All those multifarious reforms that have transformed our own working class could not even have been thought of, were in fact not thought of, until the semi-slavery of serfdom was swept away, and English labourers were given those very rights that Africans now are denied. The readers who will best understand why equality of status must precede all else are those who know the peasantry of some backward English county, among whom even now the traditions of a servile age survive. Unless directed by the squire, the parson or some other man whom money makes secure, they cannot be got to move, to form a branch of a trade union for example, or even to agree to have lamps in the road through the village. (This mental sluggishness is probably also due in part to the fact that rural England has for generations been drained of its more active-minded inhabitants, by emigration to the towns, the Colonies and America. English peasants, in fact, have slower minds than Africans.) If the minds of English peasants are still numb generations after their bonds were loosed, in how much worse case must Africans be ? As they escape

THE BACKGROUND

from the inertia to which as individuals the restraints of tribal life unconsciously condemned them, they find themselves confronted by new restraints of some of which they are conscious. Gradually they recognize that those restraints are intended to hold them back, not in the place they used to hold in their own society, but in ours, that we compelled them to enter, which they will never be able to leave. That society in Africa must for evermore be theirs as well as ours, whether they like it or not, whether we like it or not.

We should not be impatient or disappointed to learn that what people so situated most ardently want is better opportunities to get rich. You cannot expect lofty ideals in people when the one lesson we have taught them all is that they must earn money to pay the tax or go to jail, and when they are daily irked and chafed by colour bars that are intended to hinder them from advancement. Most of our own poor have no lofty ideals in life, though the wealth of all the ages is strewn around them, in books, music, the visual arts—theirs for the taking. Our poor know, if they care to enquire, that the £25 a year that it costs to educate each of their children comes mainly from the pockets of their richer countrymen. Fortunately for us, African parents in Kenya do not know, though they may suspect, that not only must they pay for their own children's education, but contribute, in taxation that is a far higher proportion of their incomes than the taxation Europeans pay, to the cost of the far better education that European children get.

CHAPTER XII

THE WAY OUT

SOME people who fully recognize the iniquity of colour bars believe that their removal must be gradual. The writer, on the contrary, believes that, as was found to be the case with Emancipation a century ago, when half-measures were tried and failed, the decisive step must be a single comprehensive affirmation by Parliament. What has emerged from the fragmentary outline contained in these pages is a recurring pattern. It is sharper in some places than in others. But it keeps turning up, so that it is no surprise to us to learn that Government expenditure on roads is 300 times more per head of the European population in the European-owned areas, than what it is in the Reserves, when we knew already that the Government spends sixty times as much on each European child's education as on each African child's education. In the writer's view it would be futile as well as foolish to try to erase that pattern in patches. Take for example the squatters' case. Suppose their colour bars dealt with one at a time, after due debate as to whether each instance of discrimination were defensible. There would be a battle over the labour code. Suppose that battle won, so that men could strike work without having to go to jail for breach of contract. That would be real gain. It might even result in the doubling of standard wage rates within a year. But it would not bring the squatters a step nearer to the one thing they all want, secure homes. They do not care, nor need we care, what legal form security should be given. Yet some law clearly would have to be passed to make squatters secure. And in the absence of any authoritative assertion of the over-riding principle by omnipotent Imperial Parliament, would it not be certain that debates in Legislatures in Africa about the kind of law that was wanted would be protracted if not worse? Nor would that be all. Even if we suppose both those battles won, it would not be long before the squatters found themselves nearly as badly off as ever. For so long as they must find 25s. or 30s. to pay the tax with, they must either work for wages or sell produce of that value. And produce cannot be sold unless the buyer can transport it to a market, and unless that market is organized. We conclude therefore that all matters of principle must be fought out in Westminster, and that Legislatures in Africa should only be concerned, under the guidance of Governors chosen for the purpose, with the practical application of principles already decided upon.

Many of the great reforms of the nineteenth century were carried out by Resolution of the Commons, that were implemented later by suitable action by the Minister responsible. That procedure has fallen into disuse. Whether by reviving it or by some other method, the essential thing is that Parliament should deliberately enact that in all the Dependencies of the Crown that are under its authority, discrimination on the ground of race, colour or religion must cease, whether in law or in administrative practice, and whether it takes the form of disabilities resting on some but not on others of a country's inhabitants, or of privileges enjoyed by some but not by others. In order to make clear what would be the practical consequences of that Resolution, the author has drafted a dispatch, for sending to the Governors of all Imperial Dependencies in Africa. In writing the dispatch he has imitated the dispatches on the same subject that were written a century ago, that were often downright and specific as State papers rarely are these days.

Before the draft is read the warning must be given that the enforcement of the policy of equal rights in British tropical Africa will arouse opposition from European minorities in Africa that will be more bitter and violent than any measure of reform has met with since Emancipation, of which that policy is our age's counterpart. To wound men's pride awakens fiercer passion than to threaten their possessions. Those of us who are most strongly convinced that wisdom as well as justice demand the re-enactment of this old British policy should also take into account the probability, so strong as to approach certainty, that its enforcement in East Africa would result in the secession of South Africa from the Empire. Coincidently there would gradually rise, in the hearts, first of a few, then of many, and in the end of the multitudes of people of African descent, wherever they live, a fountain of gratitude and loyalty, such as rose a century ago and even now has not subsided in the West Indies, despite our almost continuous neglect of those islands. The following dispatch, accordingly, assumes that by resolution or otherwise the House of Commons has explicitly directed that the policy of equal rights is to be enforced in the whole Colonial Empire.

SIR,
The recent re-affirmation by Parliament of the Imperial policy that our country first adopted over a century ago

gives me the duty of explaining the manner and scope of its application in the territory under your authority. No British Government or Parliament has ever consented to any relaxation of the policy of safeguarding the rights of a country's native inhabitants from being encroached upon by the grant of privileges to immigrants of other racial or national origin. In the case of one African country where an immigrant minority did claim a privileged position two British Governments went beyond an affirmation of equality and asserted that native interests must be paramount. While not receding from that decision, His Majesty's Government considers it enough at this juncture, in view of the doubts that are alleged to exist in certain quarters, to re-affirm and to require compliance with the principle of equality.

Misconceptions have arisen as to what this policy entails. It does not require that all a country's inhabitants must be treated with uniformity. Thus in England the law does not require all the inhabitants to contribute to the National Insurance Fund, but only employers and those they employ. Nor does the law confer the franchise on all, not even on all who have reached a certain age. And formerly, in times when the results of popular education had not yet appeared, the poorer classes were excluded from the franchise by property qualifications. In the widely different circumstances of the country you govern not only these but quite other kinds of restriction may be desirable, or even unavoidable. What the principle does exclude, and what therefore you will oppose to the extent of your powers, is any discrimination, restriction or disability, legal or administrative, on the ground of a subject's race, colour or religion. In the words of a predecessor in my office, you will withhold your consent from " those invidious distinctions referable to European and African origin, which by the mere text of the general law are abolished." It is common knowledge that in certain Dependencies such invidious distinctions have been allowed to creep into administrative practice and even into statute books. How such of them as may exist in the country you govern may best be dealt with so as to disturb vested interests as little as possible must largely rest with yourself and your advisers. But since some degree of uniformity of practice is desirable, the following observations and directions are provided for your general guidance.

The discriminations to be dealt with fall into two classes. Some privileges are of such a nature that they can, and therefore must be, either abolished or extended to all. Thus if grants of Crown land have hitherto been made to the nationals of certain countries only, to the exclusion of the nationals of certain other countries, possibly even to the exclusion of the native inhabitants, you will ensure, first that any of those last who may desire land, urban or rural, shall be able to get it on terms as favourable as those granted in the past to any others, and second, that when their demands are satisfied, the rest of the inhabitants shall be treated, in regard to grants of land, on the same footing. And if there are passages in the laws that restrict the right to own, sell, buy or lease land on either racial or religious grounds, those laws will either be amended or repealed. Similarly in regard to any franchise law that may exist. None should be disfranchised. But if the law now in force restricts the franchise on the ground of race, colour, religion or sex, you will procure its amendment. In framing such other restrictions as you may consider wise, you will be resolute in rejecting any, again to quote my predecessor, "that may perpetuate indirectly and in fact" racial discrimination. If a minority demands communal representation, and you consider the demand should properly be granted, the number of its representatives must bear the same proportion to the other elected members as the number of its electors bears to the total electorate. You will also ensure that no adult person who is literate in English is excluded from the franchise.

The other kind of discrimination is a privilege that cannot either at once be abolished or extended to the unprivileged or less privileged. That is the kind that will provide you with your hardest problems. Differences in educational opportunity are an example. We must recognize that to attempt at once to give equal opportunities to children irrespective of their racial origins would cause unjustifiable hardship. But it is equally true that delay in giving equal justice to those who now have inferior opportunities would cause hardship as unjustifiable. You will therefore set the period of five years within which the provision that your Government makes for education is to become equally available to all children. No support will be given from State funds to any new school or college entry to which is restricted on racial grounds. Existing schools with State support to which entry is restricted on racial or religious grounds will be dealt with in the following manner. You will consult the parents of the children who attend those schools, as to whether they wish both the support of the State and restricted entry to continue. If they do, you will appoint trustees to represent the racial or religious community concerned, and hand the schools over to them as free gifts. If any schools with restricted entry have hitherto been receiving support from State funds at a rate per pupil greater than the support given to other schools, that excess must be scaled down until at the end of the five-year period it ceases.

The instance of education has been chosen because, since it is in schools that equality of opportunity has in some Dependencies been most widely departed from, it will be your hardest problem. You will note that though non-Africans are richer than Africans, the directions already given will give their children a temporary advantage over African children. If in matters other than educational you consider it advisable to defer the attainment of complete equality, you will ensure that at the end of five years no discriminations on the ground of race remain.

The degree in which the policy laid down by Parliament and its implementing by the directions I have given you are relevant to the country you govern must depend on the extent to which its inhabitants have come under European influence. Where, that is to say, the old African economy still operates unchanged, except that new taxes have to be paid and that new ideas are abroad, the relevance of the policy must be small, In such conditions, for example, there can be no occasion for legislation to provide pensions or unemployment benefit. In countries, on the other hand, where most men work for wages, such protective legislation is for obvious reasons even more necessary than in Europe. I write on the assumption that in the country you govern both economies are in operation, so that many, perhaps all of the inhabitants, live partly in the old economy and partly in the new, at work for wages. I further assume that the proportion of men's lives that is spent in the new economy is increasing and will in time become total, as has happened, or is happening, in other continents. The vital decision our country has come to is that in that new economy Africans should have rights and opportunities equal with those of non-Africans, whose activities they share.

Since, however, the old African economy must in some measure persist, for a period of unknown duration, and since it must be profoundly affected by the habits and ideas learned in the new economy, some directions are added for your guidance in dealing with tribal life and institutions. It would be pleasant if we could define your duty in this regard by saying that you should leave the tribes free to determine for themselves the kind and the rate of the changes that are needed to adapt their institutions to modern conditions. I fully recognize that in existing conditions that is impossible. Yet we may go so far as my predecessor went with yours, and again urge, not only that tribes should be given real independence in local government, but also that N.A.s should be consulted beforehand about proposed legislation, should whenever possible have their wishes deferred to, and should be encouraged to translate Ordinances into their own languages. For the rest, we should recognize the fact that past experience gives us little guidance in dealing with this problem. Never before have men tried to govern wisely people who are moving, who indeed must move, out of tribal society into the world of modern industry and modern ideas, with the object of minimizing injury to the social fabric. No Governor has ever been given a task so delicate, so arduous and so important. By comparison, the controversy about discrimination may even prove less important.

The scanty records of past attempts to guide this unprecedentedly sudden passage from tribal to civilized society indicate three dangers that are avoidable, out of others that may not be. Faction can be cured only by giving people things to think about that are more interesting. African Wars of the Roses will not survive the arrival of those normal conflicts between people who see no need to change at all, and people who would leave nothing unchanged. The second danger is that in this wholly natural and salutary conflict the Government should become a partisan, or, what is as injurious, should be thought to be. The third danger arises when the rapid growth of some industry leads to inter-tribal migration, so that an area once inhabited by a single tribe comes to have a mixed population. In all such cases yours must be the choice whether room can be found for representatives of the immigrants on the N.A., or whether to abandon the tribal jurisdiction altogether, except as a voluntary association. Either of these two courses will have to be followed wherever you find that the members of one tribe are subject to the authority of some other tribe.

One section of this problem of which no solution has hitherto been found, and which therefore must be dealt with by the recipients and the writer of this dispatch, is presented by those Africans who attempt for themselves the passage from tribal to civilized society. Their very existence has hitherto been ignored. Notoriously, they throng to towns and to places with an urban character. Whatever other steps you may propose to take to provide for the needs of this rapidly growing new proletariat, I am sure you will concur in considering that such men should not be restricted to town life. They must be enabled in practice to get rural holdings, so situated as to facilitate such communal needs as water, drainage,

THE WAY OUT

schools, churches, libraries and so forth, by means of which people can replace their former involuntary tribal relations by those of their own choice. In towns, where we must expect most people who have discarded tribal ideas and habits to remain, they will of course be given equal opportunities with other residents to share in municipal and other activities.

I shall greatly value your personal observations and advice on this last range of the problems that confront us. These problems should also be a chief topic at every Governors' conference. Another topic on which I hope that Governors will advise me, both individually and collectively, is whether it is wise deliberately to interfere with the causes of the problems, whether, that is, in each particular instance, further capitalist ventures should either be prohibited or encouraged, or even subsidized.

If your difficulties are thus formidable, you will be sustained in overcoming them by the knowledge that no men in our country's history had so signal an opportunity as you and your fellow Governors now have. We have only to consider how happy it would have been if the policy outlined in these pages had been faithfully pursued in the past in Ireland and India, to see wherein your duty and mine lie in Africa now. The facts of history cannot be written afresh. But men of courage can put them to fresh uses. It is our task to ensure that in this new African era, of new associations, with the agents of Government, with employers, with teachers in schools of new facts and truths, Africans shall find themselves in a free society, in which they have opportunities to reach the best things and the highest places that are equal to those that foreigners reach and enjoy, and are subject to no restrictions other than those to which aliens are subject. There is still time to determine that when Africans awake to the knowledge of the world, and of what they like others may do in it, they will know that almost from the beginnings of their efforts to gain political liberty and liberty of mind, we welcomed and helped those efforts. Henceforth your chief aim and the chief aim of all who serve under you, explicitly avowed and pursued with confidence in its attainment, is the preparation of the whole body of the inhabitants of the country you govern for self-government.